THIRTY WRITING, SPEAKING,
AND DRAWING PROJECTS
FOR HOMESCHOOLERS

Creative
Communications

SANDRA GARANT

CATHOLIC
HERITAGE
CURRICULA

For George, who was right about the convenience of a laptop computer.

Thanks

Thank you to Cathy, Elizabeth, and Anthony Garant who agreed to have their writing samples included in this book.
They have enthusiastically tackled their writing assignments and continually offer me new ideas.

For more information:
Catholic Heritage Curricula
1-800-490-7713
www.chcweb.com

ISBN: 978-0-9788376-1-7

Other Titles by Author

A Catholic Garden of Puzzles
It's a Mystery!: The Holy Trinity
It's a Mystery!: The Perfect Personality
It's a Mystery!: The Secret Garden
It's a Mystery!: The Household of God
The Biggest Family on Earth
What Is Wealth?
Writing Workshops I-IV

Contents

Why I Wrote This Book

This book is actually a description of how and why I taught my three children to write. I read a few "teaching children how to write" books and had no desire to use the suggested exercises. They seemed meaningless and out of touch with our daily lives. I wanted my children to use writing, drawing, and speaking to handle specific situations successfully. I wanted them to be able to write conversational letters, to take phone messages, and to learn to ask thoughtful questions. I wanted them to communicate their thoughts and ideas clearly to others and to be able to determine the best means according to each situation.

If you are interested in teaching your children how to use spoken and written words and pictures like tools, then you will find meaningful ideas in this book that you can adapt to your lifestyle. This is not a weekly lesson plan on how to write good essays or five easy steps to writing haiku. Instead I want to encourage you and your children to improve your communication based upon your family's daily activities. In our house, good communication makes a more interesting and more harmonious day.

Identify Writing Opportunities

My method of teaching communication skills is to identify how we as a family need to share ideas, feelings, and facts within the family and with others. We continually turn these situations into writing, art, or public speaking projects. I usually don't follow a strict schedule, but simply select situations whenever the opportunity arises.

One of our first projects occurred accidentally. We were stuck at home one day watching the rain come down and feeling sorry for ourselves because we couldn't get out to the playground. We watched the rain for a while, and then we got out crayons and drew the rain. The activity put us in a much better mood, and we were so pleased with our pictures that we started our own

Notes:

family art gallery in the hallway with written captions under each masterpiece.

A recent family situation shows how far we have progressed. In April 1998, we bought a trampoline. Working together, the children wrote safety rules to share with our visitors. No one jumps on the trampoline without agreeing to follow the rules, which my husband and I read and approved. I gave them credit for a writing project even though the rules were their idea not mine. They wanted their friends to be safe and decided this was a good way to achieve their goal.

Not every situation has been adaptable, especially when my children were younger. Still many situations were opportunities for my husband and me to model communication skills. Our children saw us writing thank you cards, taking phone messages, giving pro-life presentations, and making lists of all kinds. Setting an example is the first step in creating a writing and public speaking environment. It's similar to parents reading aloud to children to encourage a love of reading. If parents don't write, chances are that their children won't write outside of mandatory lessons.

Why Do We Teach Writing?

Although the law requires children to learn writing, we should still ask ourselves why we want our children to be able to write well. We want them to be able to communicate with others. It's a basic survival skill.

They also need to discover when to use this skill. You don't require a saw to cut a slice of cheese. Sometimes writing is not the best way to communicate with someone. Perhaps a personal visit to a friend in the hospital would be better. Maybe a photograph sent to your faraway aunt would show how much you've grown better than a page of descriptions.

Communicating with an Audience

We can guide our young writers better if we understand that writing is a form of communication. The writer, speaker, and artist will be directing his message to an audience. Another way to state this is that words are meant to be shared with the community.

If that sounds obvious, why do many writing courses for children spend so much time on poems and fictional stories that no one except the teacher will read? Why not teach children how to take a simple telephone message? Most of us will use this form of writing more often than we will need to write poetry.

Poetry and fiction have a place in writing, but poetry and fiction in the real world also serve a purpose. They reveal truth in a memorable way, they persuade, they entertain, they celebrate.

We all need to communicate with each other and sometimes even with ourselves, as when we write reminders or to-do lists. When teaching your children how to write, speak, or draw, keep in mind that they are putting forth time and effort to create meaningful communication. I wanted my children to understand that writing is a required subject because it is a useful skill.

Notes:

Children begin communicating orally, and they need many opportunities to express themselves. By talking, they are also developing pre-writing skills. They can more easily make the transition to writing if we teach them that writing is "talking on paper." I emphasize writing throughout this book because writing is often difficult for children and because it is a required subject, unlike art and speech.

We communicate by writing and other means for various reasons—to draw attention to our needs and wants, to learn, to entertain others, to gain cooperation, to help or serve others, to identify ourselves, and to remind ourselves of information we don't want to forget. You will soon begin to see real life opportunities for writing projects; after all, we are living in the Information Age.

Where Do You Find a Community to Communicate With?

Just about anyone your child knows, doesn't know, or meets is fair game as an audience. Her dentist might enjoy getting a thank you letter, his grandparents would appreciate an original story, Dad would be impressed by a written apology, companies want to collect marketing survey and suggestion cards, or your homeschool newsletter might be accepting submissions.

Catholic Writing

Although this is not particularly a Catholic writing manual, your children will become Catholic writers by drawing from their religious experiences and by adapting the projects to their Catholic lifestyle. I don't think anyone can sincerely become a Catholic writer without first living a Catholic life.

A Brief Explanation of the Project Categories

The activities are separated into four categories: writing games, pre-writing, ready writing, and advanced writing. Both younger and older children can begin with the writing games and pre-writing projects. The games and pre-writing rely more on pictures

and speech than on written words and usually take less time to complete. Because enjoyment is a key goal of the writing games, these are valuable for laying a foundation for writing skills and for encouraging reluctant writers.

If your children are already writing, but you are not pleased with their ability, try adapting the pre-writing projects and the writing games to motivate them to extra effort in their writing. A twelve year old who writes place cards for a Knights of Columbus dinner begins to appreciate the value of both legible handwriting and writing something meaningful. By writing someone's name, she is improving the organization and flow of an event. When creating riddles either orally or in writing for family and friends to solve, children gain confidence in their ability to think and to express their unique vision. They don't want to give the answer away too soon, so they pay attention to the order of their clues.

The ready writing projects are also adaptable and can be done individually or as a group. Most of these projects require complete sentences, some spelling skills, and more creativity. Many of the writing games are also appropriate for this level. Some of the games challenge children to develop interesting and complex sentences and to order their thoughts according to a specific pattern, such as concentrating on sounds or on giving complete directions.

The last group of projects takes more time, planning, research, and writing or public speaking skills. I directly address the writer in these projects because the main purpose of this book is to develop mature writers who know how to communicate well in various situations. Writing becomes less of a lesson and more of a skill that he knows when, where, and how to use without being told. Writing, drawing, and public speaking begin to merge naturally with the writer's personal challenges, relationships, responsibilities, and activities.

I am not implying that a teen's writing should be secretive. Parents still have a role in supervising the projects in the last section. By this stage, however, the writer should be able to make most of the decisions as to when and how to use writing and the other forms of communication in his everyday life. Maybe none of the last projects will appeal to your teen, but he will find other motivating reasons for communicating.

Resources:

The four appendices list additional information or resources for several of the projects, particularly the ones that require advanced skills. For instance, the writer may want technical help with the last project. He may turn to Appendix Two for video production how to books.

The last section of the book contains writing samples from my three children. They cover a wide range of communication—true stories, letters, a play, a list used for tax records, answering machine scripts, a proposal, prayer petitions, and even my daughter's last will and testament. Several of the items were not originally assignments. The samples are not completely corrected because of the age and grammar level of the authors at the time of the writing. I hope that these samples may inspire you to develop even more writing activities. The projects, games, and samples described in this manual certainly do not cover all the possibilities.

You should not have to worry about thinking up assignments every week for your children, especially the older ones. After a few months, your children should be coming to you with their own suggestions for earning writing credit. Why not let them autograph and write a short message on the end paper of a book given as a gift—after you have okayed a rough draft on regular writing paper? I also borrow ideas from other people and the normal course of events. For example, our parish Confirmation program required a written paragraph from each confirmand. The grandparents oblige by sending gifts that require thank yous, and New Year's Day is set aside for Mass and reflecting on resolutions or goals for the new year.

Reluctant Writers

The Infrequent Balker

If your child sometimes balks at writing, the problem could be that she is simply tired. Perhaps she doesn't understand your instructions, or nothing is "happening", meaning she has writer's block. Some days, I sit at the keyboard and nothing "happens" for an hour. On other days, I can write several pages in half an hour. When there is nothing to say, it is usually best for the writer or speaker to say nothing.

However, you can often remedy writer's block. Take a break from writing for a few minutes by talking or stretching. Repeat the instructions if necessary. Do something else that engages the senses, such as listening to music, building with blocks, or cooking for 15 to 30 minutes. Playing "Connect the Words," "Switch It," or "Moving Pencils" from the Writing Games section can kick start the mind into writing again. The idea is not to give up, but to connect the writing to your common experience. Writing does not occur in a vacuum—it requires connection with something that we know or are experiencing.

Untangle the Real Story by Listening

If an older child is having trouble with any writing project, suggest that you talk about the subject together. Then let him do most of the talking. Let him tell you the "story" of his trouble with writing.

You don't have to know anything about the subject, and it doesn't have to be a fictional story. I write nonfiction material, and I talk either to myself or to my family.

You may get complaints at first, but be patient. Writing can be frustrating. Usually children will talk themselves past "I don't want to do this, and I can't do this" to "I don't know where to start" or "I don't know how to put it together" if you listen long enough.

If they are stalled with their feelings of frustration, begin to question them slowly. "Do you like the beginning? Is that where

you want to start?" Ask them if they understand where the project should end. Maybe they don't know the reason for the writing, and so they have no focus.

Perhaps the real problem is the organization of the material. Maybe the writing is too brief or too wordy. Maybe they became tangled in their own words. Possibly they need more information or experience. The project could be too difficult for their present skill level.

The Dedicated Non-writers

If an older child seldom wants to write, he might not understand the power behind this skill. Give him easy opportunities to learn that writing is powerful. He can make that discovery on his own if you stop the writing lessons and integrate very small writing projects into his daily life maybe two or three times a week. "Very small" and "daily life" are the key words here.

He probably won't realize that he is writing when you ask him to put together a grocery list, to jot down some ideas for your next vacation, and to help his little sister create a birthday card for Grandma. Ask him to proofread a letter you wrote by saying "Do you think I left anything important out? Should I use a different word here? What would be your reaction to receiving a letter like this?" The grammar is not the point of proofreading here, especially if he doesn't have confidence in his spelling or grammar skills. Always show your appreciation of the writing he finishes.

Another strategy is to write to him about things that you know are important to him. You can write a list of what you like best about him and leave it on his pillow or slide it under his breakfast plate. You can write a poem to celebrate his basketball victory or a cartoon giving him permission to keep that garter snake he found in the garden as a pet. Write telephone messages for him when he's not available to come to the phone. Set a good example for him. Show him realistic ways to use writing and other communication skills.

He will begin to understand eventually, and then you can suggest more detailed writing projects when an appropriate occasion for writing arises.

Keep The Projects Reasonable

After reading writing books that suggest a child spend an hour perfecting "An Ode to My Toothbrush" or "An Epitaph to a Chocolate Chip Cookie", I agree with children who are reluctant to write if these are the usual subjects. I think they are being reasonable. Some of us have nothing to say to our toothbrushes.

Most of us should be able to find enough reasonable motivation to write or use other communication skills every day. We all have responsibilities we need to remember, relationships we want to keep, problems we ought to resolve, interests we would like to explore, and celebrations in which we enjoy participating. These are meaningful and therefore motivating opportunities for writing, speaking, and drawing.

Resources:

Writing Games

What am I?

Subjects

1. Familiar items differing in function, shape, and color

   a. Eraser

   b. Pencil

   c. Globe

   d. Crayons

   e. Scissors

2. Photos of animals or people

3. Items of the same color, material, or function

   a. Toys

   b. Drawing materials

   c. Blue items

   d. Metal items

4. Numbers or Letters, Countries or Cities, Foods

Details are necessary for good writing. Give children a chance to write riddles that depend upon finding and describing details.

Writing lists:

How to Play

Assemble the subjects. Begin by reading the examples below or by making up a riddle based on a subject on the table. Describe the color, size, function, and a distinguishing characteristic of the subject. The child guesses the answer. Then the child chooses a subject and gives at least *three* clues orally. End with the phrase "What Am I?" This is the signal for guessing to begin.

Depending upon the age of the child, continue the lesson as a written assignment either the same day or the following day. Post all riddles for children to read and guess if you are working with a group. Children will enjoy writing riddles for family members, too. They could send these in e-mails or in regular letters to relatives and friends.

I am thin. I'm made of wood but not my middle. I usually get shorter and shorter. I go with paper. What am I? (a pencil)

I am brown and heavy. I have four legs, but I am not alive. I am underneath you. What am I? (a chair)

I live in a box. I am not alive. Don't eat me, but you can unwrap me. I am round but not like a ball. I am red. What am I? (a red crayon)

I am yellow. I am not a t-shirt. I am not a piece of paper. What am I? [These clues were not enough. The child had to give additional clues.] I am not inside a house. I am very hot. Don't look at me. What am I? (The Sun)

I am a number between 10 and 20. I can be divided [evenly] by 4. If you add my [digits], you get an answer of 7. What number am I? (16)

Sound Off!

Writing can be noisy! Movies and poems and stories can all use sound effects to make the action more interesting. Sometimes the sound effects are obvious and sometimes they are hidden.

How to Play

Read *We're Going on a Bear Hunt* by Helen Oxenbury for ages 3-8 and "The Bells" by Edgar Allan Poe for ages 9 and up. Point out the sound words if necessary. If you have photocopies of the noisy writing, the children can go on a treasure hunt to circle the noisy words. Once the children have their attention drawn to the sound words, try the remaining activities orally at first and then in writing.

Children can take turns contributing to a master list of sound words. This list will be used in sound games that follow. Either write the words on the chalkboard or have the children write the words in their notebooks for future reference.

If appropriate for the age group of your students, introduce the term "onomatopoeia," which describes words that imitate or are associated with natural sounds.

Cock-a-doodle-do

Bow-wow

Meow

Whoosh

Plop

Resources:

13

Story-telling

Read a short story such as a fable or fairy tale. Aesop's fables are perfect for this activity. Each child takes a turn making a sound that fits with the story. Pause for three seconds when a sound would be appropriate. Children must pay attention and be ready for the pauses. If they take too long or aren't paying attention, they lose their turn and the next sound opportunity goes to the next child or continue with the story.

Have the children re-write a familiar story or poem adding their own sounds. Children should have the story or poem in front of them before beginning. They may use the master sound list.

Red Riding Hood walked through the forest to her grandmother's house. La, la, la. She picked a flower. Pluck. The wolf spotted her. Yum! Slick, slick! He licked his chops. He ran ahead and laughed quietly. Ha, ha, ha. He found the grandmother's house and snap! ate her up. He put on her hat and glasses and got under the covers. Knock! Red Riding Hood arrived. He told her to come in. She came in and thought her grandmother looked strange. Hmmm. Oh no! The wolf jumped up and chased her. A woodman came to the rescue. Whack! He killed the wolf. Whew!

Tell or read a story using voice as a sound effect. How can the voice sound dreadful, enthusiastic, sorrowful, or suspicious?

Hide and Seek

This game gives children practice writing details and directions.

How to Play

Ask children for good hiding places in the area around them if they shrank to the size of one inch. List the places they name. Then ask them to describe each hiding place without naming it directly. For example, if the desk is a hiding place, they describe the desk without calling it a desk. "I'm hiding in a flat box on legs." "I'm hiding inside a metal thing that has old paper in it" might refer to the wastepaper basket.

With two or more children, have each child or group write clues that lead to a treasure. The children trade clues in order to search for the treasure. The easiest way to do this is to have the children working in different rooms or at different times. Decide on the treasure beforehand. The treasure might be a favorite story, a game the children enjoy playing, stickers, cookies, etc.

Connect the Words

Stories often rely on connecting things together in new or unexpected ways.

How to Play

Ask the children to imagine how two different things could possibly become connected in a story. The purpose is not to tell a story, but to think of a situation. In order to connect things, details need to be added to explain the connection. These details can make the story much more interesting.

Subjects

Goldfish and coffee

Elephants and ballerinas

Poetry and motorcycles

Farmer and a boat

Goats and an opera singer

A palace and a bale of hay

Cell phone and pirate

A soldier and a mouse

Bread and shoes

An alligator and a piano

Cheese and a football

Children may think of new subjects to combine and write these down. Each child picks several from the list and writes two possibilities for each combination.

Ask the children to recall and describe a memory. Can they also remember any information about sights, sounds, tastes, smells, or emotions connected with this memory?

Location, Location, Location

Stories take place in specific settings or locations. If the setting is important to the story, the writer should describe it. In this game, the location is important because the writer wants to be rescued and must give directions to the rescuer.

Stories also explain causes and effects. The reader will want to know why the writer needs rescuing, so the writer should give explanations.

How to Play

Children examine a globe or a map and choose a location to become stranded. They must explain how they got to this location and how they became stranded. Then they must give clues using geographical terms to describe where they are. Finally they must request assistance and one or more items they would like their rescuers to bring them.

You may actually want to put the messages in a bottle and pull them out to read and figure out the locations. Here are some examples:

Help! I was riding my red jet ski and having fun. I was riding a long time. I went all over in the Caribbean Sea until I ran out of gas in a country south of Cuba. This country is not an island. It is west of Venezuela. Please bring me gasoline so I can get back home.

Help! I was on a big boat looking at whales, and a whale swallowed the whole boat. But the whale sneezed me out. I swam to an island in the Pacific. It's near the Tropic of Cancer and directly west of Mexico City. Please bring me a bottle of water and gum. Thank you.

HELP!!! I was fishing in the ocean and a wave washed me overboard. I swam to an island that is a state and has palm trees. I landed in a palm tree. I would like some strawberries.

Notes:

16

What if you needed to call for help from home? How could you give directions to your house?

Number Pyramid

Writing must have an organization. Organization helps the reader follow the information. If the reader can't follow the story line, then she may stop reading or misunderstand the story. We don't read books backwards, do we?

Information can be organized in many different ways. Using numbers is one way to build suspense and organize information. Here are two examples:

> One dog growling,
> Two cats purring,
> Three bears sleeping,
> Four lions hunting,
> Five horses galloping,
> Six farmers plowing,
> Seven kings fighting—
> All drawn in my picture books.

> One drummer,
> Two flags,
> Three horses,
> Four clowns,
> Five balloons,
> Six old cars,
> Seven bands,
> Nine hundred people
> watching a parade.

How to Play

Discuss what things would be on a list at these places: A circus, a basketball game, a street, a city, a bookstore, a restaurant, a church, the universe. How can you group the things by numbers?

Choose a favorite story or movie. Can you describe it by using this method? For example: One poor widow, one boy, five beans,

one long climb, one giant, two bags of gold, one brown hen, one singing harp, one axe, and no more giant.

Directional Challenge

Giving clear directions is important and yet not always easy. This game will improve your child's ability to give accurate directions and to listen carefully. You need at least two players for this game. One player looks at the mystery shapes below and gives oral directions to the second player on how to draw the unseen shape. Once a direction is given and the drawer has begun, the speaker may correct the direction using only words (not gestures) if the drawer has misunderstood or if the directions were not clear. When the drawing is finished, compare the original with the copy.

Once you have played the game using the two given shapes, create your own simple drawings to continue playing. You may use directional terms, such as north and south or left and right. Describing geometrical shapes and the location of the shape on the paper will become necessary. "Draw a circle" usually isn't enough. The drawer needs to know how big the circle should be and where it should be placed on the paper. Discovering how to describe and instruct the drawer is part of the fun of this game.

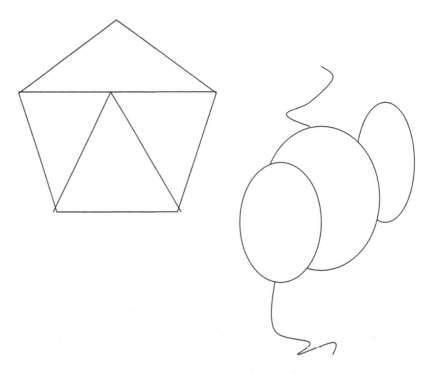

Sentence Stretching

Children have a tendency to write very short sentences that give little information. To move away from "I like my mom, I like my dad, and they like me," try this game. The winner is the writer with the longest sentence. This exaggeration will help the children see that they can write longer, more interesting sentences. Not every sentence should be exaggerated in length, but a variety of sentence lengths will hold the reader's interest and enhance the quality of the writing.

How to Play

Write one of the following sentences on paper or a chalkboard. Ask the children to stretch the sentence. What can they add or change to give more information, to paint a word picture? If necessary, ask prompting questions: What kind of a dog? What was the dog's name? When? Where? Why? How high?)

The dog jumped.

Tom is fishing.

We like ice cream.

Mary sings.

The children ran.

The horse is tiny.

The rain fell.

Children may choose a sentence and have two minutes to stretch it in writing. Word changes are permitted as long as the basic meaning is the same. For instance, "Charles giggled" may be changed to "Charles's sides hurt because he laughed for two days." Who wrote the longest sentence?

We are writing.

Don't shout.

The books arrived.

I have a pet elephant.

The vulture soared.

The police officer drove.

Put this on the table.

The children smiled.

The shark swam.

The wind blew.

Switch It

Word choice is important. Writers may spend time exchanging one word for another or rewriting sentences to change the meaning slightly.

How to Play

Below are altered titles of movies and books. Can you determine the correct titles?

The Dreadful-looking Baby Duck (The Ugly Duckling)

The Urban Rodent and the Rural Rodent (City Mouse and Country Mouse)

Constellation Conflicts (Star Wars)

The Aristocrat of the Circles (The Lord of the Rings)

The Breeze through the Trees (The Wind in the Willows)

Fortune Atoll (Treasure Island)

The Appeal of the Untamed (The Call of the Wild)

Give children an opportunity to alter the titles of books. Place the books on a table for them to see. Then read the titles aloud. A dictionary or thesaurus to look up synonyms and spellings will be helpful.

Shakespeare's Words

(ages 10 and up)

William Shakespeare chose his words wisely. Make changes to one of the following passages by substituting synonyms for at least four words. The word choice will change the meaning and the rhythm.

Is this a dagger which I see before me,

The handle toward my hand? Come, let me clutch thee.

I have thee not, and yet I see thee still. (*Macbeth*)

My grief lies all within,

And these external manners of lament

Are merely shadows to the unseen grief

That swells with silence in the tortured soul. (*Richard II*)

Give every man thy ear, but few thy voice.

Take each man's censure, but reserve thy judgment.

Costly thy habit as thy purse can buy,

But not express'd in fancy; rich, not gaudy;

For the apparel oft proclaims the man; (*Hamlet*)

Resources:

Moving Pencils

Many students abandon their writing within seconds after beginning. They allow themselves to get distracted, or they simply pick up their pencils and stop writing.

How to Play

Children should write the subject at the top of a sheet of paper. Then set a timer for two minutes and start writing about the subject. Children may not lift their pencil from the paper, stop writing, or look around. If a child cannot think of anything to write, he simply writes "I can't think of anything to write about (whatever the subject is.)" until time is up or he thinks of something else to add about the subject. The subject is simply a place to start. Children can change the subject at any time as long as they keep writing.

Increase the time to a maximum of five to ten minutes when the child has tried the two-minute time period at least three times. Children are often surprised at how much they are able to write once they keep their pencils moving.

Subjects

Ripe icy cold watermelon

A tall sandcastle with a flag

An angry barking black dog

A roaring red motorcycle

A steamy bowl of chicken soup

A tree house with a rope ladder

A tired sweaty runner

A worm on a fishhook

A baseball player at bat

A boat on a stormy sea

2

DRAWING

Pre-writing Projects

Creating an Environment for Success

God created an environment for man to live in before He expected man to begin living. In the same way, parents need to create an environment for children to communicate in before children begin communicating with words. If this environment is missing, your children may try to communicate by talking, writing, or drawing, but their efforts will be frustrated. It would be hard for an adult to write without paper and pencil or a word processor regardless of ability.

Briefly, pre-writers require time and attention from parents (or another audience, such as grandparents, brothers, sisters, etc.), examples of communication from others, and paper and crayons or pencil. They need to be listened to, and they need a chance to play with words, paper, and pencil.

Although children do write a little at this stage, I call it "pre-writing" because it's more of a preparation for writing, and because separating the stages gives children and parents evidence of progress. But move back and forth between the projects when the need arises in your family.

For instance, our family still makes signs, which is a pre-writing project. We discovered we needed a sign for the back door to indicate when someone was playing with the rabbits so that another family member wouldn't accidentally let the dog out,

creating much chaos and possibly a death scene in our normally tranquil backyard. Rabbits can die of fright, so we'd like to protect them with the help of a sign.

The emphasis at this stage really should be a sense of play, exploration, and discovery. You want your children not only to play with communication but to discover its advantages and rewards, such as harmony and peace between a dog and rabbits.

Spelling and Grammar Mistakes?

During the pre-writing phase, I didn't worry about spelling mistakes unless the situation would have created public embarrassment for my children. No one expects a five year old to be able to spell "refrigerator", but most four or five year olds can learn to spell their name and family names correctly.

When children understand that they are writing something that others will pay attention to, they usually want to spell well for the sake of their readers. I preferred to spell words on a need to know basis at this age. You can formally begin to teach spelling during the pre-writing projects or wait until later.

Once a child is able to print letters without too much labor, you can slowly add grammar rules. A child can concentrate better if you don't throw too many new skills at him in the beginning.

Writing his name might be difficult enough, so don't insist that he capitalize until his writing becomes more automatic. My children learned all the small letters first when they began to write. Their first grammar lesson was on capitalization. Appendix Four contains a list of simple grammar rules.

Word Games

We did and still do play spelling and word games for fun and to improve our ability to handle words. You may have your own favorites. We'd like to share a few of ours.

An Adjective Game

We play "The Minister's Cat", which we learned while watching Scrooge starring Albert Finney. Each player recites "The Minister's Cat is a — cat" filling in the blank with one adjective describing the cat alphabetically in turn. So player one might say "The minister's cat is an arrogant cat", player two "The minister's cat is an agile cat", and player three "The minister's cat is an angry cat". When every player has had a turn, player one moves on to adjectives beginning with the letter "B"—perhaps the cat is now a bold cat according to player one and a befuddled cat in the mind of player two. No one may repeat an adjective once it is used. If you have a mixed group, you can rule that older children must use adjectives of more than one syllable, while younger ones can give simple, single syllable adjectives.

A Memory Game

Another game we liked was called "One Wonderful Whale Whistles". Children play with sounds, parts of speech, rhythm, and memorization during this game. Player one begins the alliteration working up the number line, saying "One wonderful whale whistles" or any other combination that works with the sound "w", such as "One wacky watchman winks". Player two goes to the next number, creating a new alliterative sentence and then repeats all previous sentences from memory. "Two tiny twins talk, and one wonderful whale whistles." We usually play up to ten, although sometimes we begin at ten with a phrase like "Ten terrible tyrants testify" and count our way down to the one wonderful whale whistling.

Spelling on the Road

When we are in the car, sometimes the children take turns spelling road signs. My son will spy a sign that says "Groceries", and he spells it before we go past since he doesn't know how to spell "groceries" from memory. I ask them not to spell brand names, but "yield", "speed limit", "hospital", and other information words come in handy.

You could make a case for learning how to spell "Kentucky Fried Chicken"®, since Kentucky is a state, but "Exxon"® and "Dunkin Donuts"® are expendable. If you are taking a long trip, this game does teach quite a few words, and the whole family can play. You can look for unusual words, food words (which does make the kids hungry), verbs, or only words beginning with a certain letter.

Resources:

25

Spelling Programs

We use Davidson's *Spell-It* computer software, which you can customize with some time and trouble. It doesn't contain words we sometimes want to know, and we haven't found the time to customize ours with essential Catholic terms. You must write several sentences and misspellings for each word you want to add, and I haven't found a way to locate specific words to see if they are already listed. We began using the spelling software when my youngest was about nine. The children use it occasionally because the games are fun.

My Catholic Speller written by Nancy Nicholson fills the need for introducing necessary Catholic words to our children's spelling lists. The weekly lesson plans are easy to use and not overwhelming. The price is right too. Mrs. Nicholson's grammar program *Language of God for Little Folks* is very affordable and also provides spelling and grammar practice using Catholic words.

Rhythm Spelling

A technique for musically inclined children is to spell words in rhythm, preferably the same rhythm each time. The word "spelling" for example can be spelled "s,p—e,double l—i,n,g". "Communion" is spelled "c,o,m—m,u,n—i,o,n" at our house. Try to keep vowel and consonant blends together, as well as suffixes and prefixes, unless the rhythm doesn't work. For example, the word "prepare" has the prefix "pre" and the root "pare", so that would be a logical division. My children's favorite word is "icicle" because the rhythm— "i,c—i,c—l,e"—is memorable, although the suffix "cle" is broken.

Spelling, like grammar, is for the convenience of the readers. Spelling and grammar make writing understandable, in the same way that legible handwriting and clear copies make writing readable.

Project 1:
Introducing . . .

Teach your child how to introduce herself to strangers who come to visit. (A stranger is anyone your child doesn't know or doesn't remember.) Why? Because communication often begins with an introduction. Many books begin with an introduction. Conversations usually begin with some kind of introduction, such as "Hello" or "Excuse me".

Sometimes children are shy because they don't know what to say to those huge people hovering over them. They may have something to communicate orally, but getting started for writers and conversationalists can be difficult. Many of us are intimidated by size, and discovering that you can use polite introductions to break into a subject is encouraging. Help your child to discover the power and the form of an introduction.

"Hello, my name is Sandra, and I'm glad to meet you" is all they need to say unless their name is Julie or Mary. We also encourage our children to shake hands firmly with guests as part of the introduction.

Name Tags

If you know you are about to meet strangers, write your child's name on a name tag, or let him write it. I encouraged mine to introduce themselves, but I had one who was extremely shy and needed time to get acquainted. A shy child can point to her name tag instead of getting completely left out of the introduction.

Some children just like to wear name tags whether or not they are meeting people. If you want them to practice writing their names, you might invest in an inexpensive roll of name stickers. They can wear a new name tag every day. My children loved it.

Readers of name tags will often give your children feedback, which is important for aspiring writers. Children will soon grasp the idea that their readers must be able to decipher their writing.

Communicating Common Courtesy

I have noticed that adults are delighted when children introduce themselves properly. After an introduction, they tend to include the children more frequently in the general conversation. Some adults have trouble talking to children. Name tags and polite oral introductions break down communication barriers.

In contrast, I have also seen adults struggle and give up on a conversation with a child who doesn't attempt to respond. At the end of a regional spelling bee, a group of children stood limply in front of a judge. He tried to congratulate them individually by speaking to them and shaking their hand. About 90% of the children did not make eye contact and had to have their hand grasped while it was still hanging by their side. The judge was getting frustrated, but he had limited options in such a public situation.

Your child could turn into a brilliant writer and be a poor conversationalist, but good communication often requires listening to and engaging in dialogue with others whether we are speaking face-to-face or writing e-mails to each other half a world away.

Project 2:
Labeling Games

Fun with Visitors

This is a variation of Project 1 where your child identifies familiar and sometimes unfamiliar people with name tags. Again, the primary purpose is a proper introduction. It is easier to talk to someone if you know his name, and these name tags also serve as small gifts.

After all, words are meant to be shared with others. Writers need readers. Very young writers need understanding friendly readers who recognize how long and lovingly they have labored to form the letters that say "Grandma" or "Ganma" or however the complex masterpiece turns out.

Grandma, Grandpa, and Uncle Joseph will probably be delighted to play along and wear their own homemade name tag when they come to visit. Grandmas have even been known to cherish these homemade gifts from their adoring fans and save them in scrapbooks.

If you have guests coming for a visit, your child can write name tags for everyone and offer the identification at the time of introduction. It's a simple way to get young children ready to meet new people. When our children began voice lessons at home in January 2000, they made name tags for themselves for the first two visits to help the instructor learn their names. He properly told them that he didn't want to point!

Another possibility is to write name cards for the table so your guests will know where to sit. Unruled index cards folded in half are handy for this project. You can offer to do this as a service project with your older children for your parish or a charitable organization. If your child learns or knows calligraphy, you'll soon find lots of opportunities for serving others by writing names neatly on certificates for various events, such as Baptisms.

Everything In Its Place

When I was trying to learn Spanish, the book I used had hundreds of stickers that I was supposed to label objects with. Every time I looked at the table, I would see "mesa".

If you don't mind the "mesa" it will create, you can let your aspiring writer and speller loose with labels in the house or in his bedroom. Match the size of his handwriting with the size of the labels. Maybe the assignment can be two or three labels a day.

Younger and older children can permanently label a variety of objects, such as folders, the clean laundry basket, the dirty laundry basket, clothing, the pencil cup, the dog's collar or leash, containers for nails, plant stakes, the garbage can, their bedroom door, and whatever else you want labeled for better organization or in the hopes of having it returned when lost.

I wouldn't set a six year old at liberty with a black permanent marker, but you can use paint, stencils, crayons, stickers, washable markers, colored pencils, wood-burning tools, and many other writing instruments. Usually, we use whatever is closest to hand if it seems that it will work for the project.

Project 3: Signs

You may not realize how badly you need a sign for the front door, but my guess is that you do need one. You might need a verse of Scripture neatly written so that people waiting for you to answer the door have something to read. Maybe you need to warn people to "Beware of Dog". You might politely give notice that you would prefer not to be bothered by door-to-door salesmen. I'm volunteering your children for these necessary jobs.

My children are trying to persuade me that we need a sign for the backyard that says "Patio Cafe", but first we need to find an outdoor table. My son is convinced we would have more birds eating out of his homemade birdfeeder if I let him put a sign near it saying "Free Birdseed".

Maybe you need a "Garage Sale" sign, a "Happy Birthday!" sign, a "Family Reunion Here" sign, or how about a "Homeschoolers' Choir Meeting" sign?

Signs don't generally require a lot of writing, and yet they communicate in a large and exciting way from a child's perspective. Many signs have a high degree of importance to children simply because they are large but also because they often generate reactions from the readers. Little authors are aware of this and will ask anxiously, "Did you see my sign?"

Sign Designing

Perhaps you have a situation where a sign would educate or warn the public. Begin with scratch paper and lay out the lettering for your rough draft. (Don't neglect the scratch paper stage because you are also introducing your children to the idea of rough drafts and final drafts for writing projects.)

Have your children stand at a distance and check the size of the lettering. Ask them if it should be larger or smaller? Will people be able to read it easily? Do the letters look neat? (Once they have answered the above questions, they have evaluated or proofread their work.) Very young children won't be concerned

about centering the letters, but you can show older children how to use a ruler to straighten and center the line of lettering on scratch paper.

If the rough draft is acceptable, choose the materials for your final version. You can use scrap lumber, fabric, paint, markers, wood-burning tools, stencils, and vinyl letters to create weatherproof or weather resistant signs. You can draw light pencil guidelines on the permanent signboard to keep the letters neat and even when you are writing or sticking them on.

Quoting the Words of Others

I mentioned writing a Scripture verse, which is technically copying, but it's also technically quoting, and you can teach your child from an early age to cite the source and use quotation marks. As your children get older, they can learn to write to publishers for copyright permission for pictures or words.

Material may be paraphrased but not reproduced paragraph after paragraph without written permission. See Appendix Three for more information on copyrights.

Project 4: Picture and Oral Letters

My children enjoyed the daily ritual of going to the mailbox. Maybe it seemed like a treasure hunt to them. They liked to collect the stamps and open the envelopes. Then they wanted to know why the mail was addressed to Mom and Dad and why they rarely got any.

Leaving the issue of junk mail until they were older, I explained that they had to write letters if they wanted people to write back to them. But they didn't know how to write! Well, it was time for someone to get educationally creative, and so we came up with two ideas—oral letters and picture letters.

Both types of letters help children discover and explore communication, and depending on the situation, they can teach good manners, stimulate creativity, and improve speech skills.

Oral Letters

Tape record a "letter" from your child to a friend or relative. Explain to your child that the tape recording machine copies his voice. Let him recite the alphabet or a familiar song or prayer to find out what he sounds like if he isn't used to the idea of using a recorder.

Once your child understands that his voice will be copied, suggest that you send a special message to whomever you have chosen. It helps to have a real purpose for the message, such as a thank you for a gift or a Happy Birthday greeting.

If a young child is not able to carry on much of a conversation, you can record a dialogue. You ask the right questions and your child answers. For example, if you are sending a Happy Birthday greeting to Aunt Jane, you might begin with the question, "Do you know what happens on August 8th?" If your child gets tongue-tied, it's okay to ask leading questions. "Is it someone's birthday?" "What would you like to say to Aunt Jane on her birthday?"

Notes:

Tape recorded letters can be set up like written letters with the date, address, and a salutation, or you may choose to record an informal conversation between all the family members with each person giving a personal message. You can close with a favorite song, poem, or prayer.

As your children get older, they may choose more creative programs for their oral letters. These will probably require a written script unless your child is skillful at improvising. They might write a personal poem to thank Grandpa for a fishing trip. "Perch are yellow, the water is blue, I sure do like going fishing with you!"

A message set up as a radio dispatch would be interesting. You could use your address or phone number as the call letters. "This is Smith 111-2222. Do you copy, Uncle Bob? Stand by for a high priority message."

You could send an invitation to a family get together in the form of a radio ad. "Coming to you pre-recorded from the Garant Family Studios is your host George with a special invitation." Or why not send a singing telegram? Our children sang "Happy Birthday" and "For She's a Jolly Good Fellow" with a Cockney accent for a family friend one year. One family we know allows their eight year old to record messages for their telephone answering machine.

Speaking on tape can improve a child's awareness of pronunciation. Some teenagers and adults mumble and do not properly pronounce words when speaking. It's almost painful to listen to them. They tend to speak sloppily, which negatively influences their audience. If your teenager is afraid to speak in public, practicing with a tape recorder can increase his confidence.

Picture Letters

Not all children will be interested in sending oral letters. They might prefer to draw picture letters instead. Perhaps your son received a birthday gift by mail, but he's too young to send a thank you letter. Ask him to draw a picture of the gift. You can write "Thank you" and let him write the proper name of the gift giver.

Perhaps you wish to invite someone for a visit. Your child can draw a picture of the family or the family home, and you write the actual invitation. Using picture letters, you can thank someone for their visit or their hospitality while you were visiting.

Let young children use postcards or small notecards. Their first letters don't have to be long-winded. An index card is not as difficult for a young writer to fill up as a standard piece of paper.

Maybe all your child can write is his name or the first three letters of the alphabet. Well, that's enough for a homemade picture postcard sent to Dad. We would often send short letters to my husband at work or put them in his lunchbox. The children enjoyed it, and he certainly didn't mind getting personal mail.

Communication Preferences

Each one of my children has a different communication preference. Our goal is to get the message to our audience clearly and charitably. You may discover that one of your children enjoys drawing and writing and that another is more enthusiastic about telephone calls or tape-recorded letters. Most children will naturally gravitate toward one form of communication. As they become skilled at their natural preference, your children will gain confidence and an awareness of the strengths and limitations of their preferences. Encourage them to try other possibilities when necessary.

A young man who turned to writing because of his speech impediment remarked that writing freed his words. He will probably never be completely comfortable with public speaking, but he communicates beautifully through his poetry. On the other hand, a college acquaintance of mine simply couldn't write. It was an ordeal to evaluate his written work, but he surprised and pleased our communication class by giving a brilliant, improvised speech.

Although the above two examples are extreme, you may notice more subtle contrasts in your own children. These are normal. Not all of us will be distinguished artists, although most of us can learn to draw for those occasions that seem most suited for communicating with a picture. Give your children opportunities to explore various forms of communication. Permit them to mix art with words or an improvised speech and tape recording. Their communication will be more interesting, and they and their audience will enjoy the process.

Resources:

Project 5: Storytelling

What do you do when you have a houseful of children and the power goes out? No, you don't panic. You take turns telling stories to each other. Actually, don't wait for the power to go out. Telling stories is too much fun and educational to wait that long.

Before books and movies, storytelling was a vital part of education and entertainment for families and communities. Christ communicated many important truths through parables. Storytelling is part of our heritage.

Maybe you do not consider yourself a storyteller. But you are full of stories, the kind of stories your children would like to hear and should hear.

Set a Telling Example

Tell your children stories about your own childhood. Think about something that happened to you. When did you learn to swim? Did you ever break any bones? How about the time you dropped eggshell in the cake batter and didn't notice until someone remarked how crunchy the cake was at supper? What kind of pets did you have? How did you spend Sunday afternoons?

If you still can't get going on a good story, open a family photo album and tell a story based upon the contents. "These were our Easter dresses. That's Aunt Jean and Aunt Debbie and me in the middle. We're fidgeting because it's hot, and we're ready to go hunt eggs. Your Grandma made us new Easter dresses every year . . ." My children's first history lessons were family stories like these. They were fascinated and often asked me to tell them again the story about when I broke my arm. Most families have more than one photo album that will provide many historical family facts.

When you run out of true stories, make up stories with your children as the heroes. I wrote these down for my children and included their friends in some of the stories. They still re-read these.

You can re-tell parables and Bible stories. Storytelling is not the same as story reading. It creates a different experience. Storytelling exercises our memories and our ability to think

quickly and logically. Children won't be harsh critics, especially if you begin when they are young. If you are having difficulty coming up with plot ideas, turn to appendix one.

Taking Turns

There is a time to talk and a time to listen. Now it is your child's turn to tell his stories. Instead of asking your child to tell a full-blown story, first give him a chance to explain, describe, and re-tell. When we are traveling in the car, I sometimes ask my children to look for pictures in the clouds. Younger children will be intrigued by the game and are sometimes more creative than older children. Perhaps you will get comments like "That cloud looks like an angel riding a horse." If not, set an example and ask them if they can see the duck chasing a pig.

Let them re-tell jokes and riddles. This must be a stage most children go through anyway. Each one of mine has simply done this without any prompting. I just had to be a willing audience. I took advantage of it, encouraging them not to read the jokes from the book but to "tell it to me on your own."

Let them slop around in the mud and play with crickets. Children need experiences before they can tell about the experiences in a story. So when they are excited about the way the frog's skin feels, try not to back off but let them describe their excitement and discovery. Storytelling is sometimes a messy, sweaty experience. Don't let the frog incident go to waste once you've suffered through it. The next time they write or tape record a letter, suggest they tell the story about the frog. Maybe it would make a great beginning for a fiction story.

Once your children are comfortable describing and re-telling, you can begin a story and ask them to make up a good ending. However, mine thought I already had an ending in mind and begged to know how the story was supposed to end. Let them know that you are going to tell a story together because you have a good beginning, but you are stuck for a good ending.

As my children got better at storytelling, we came up with a more difficult version. One person started the story and got the characters into a terrible jam. He immediately handed over the story to the next person who had to get them out of trouble and set them up with new problems. We survived airplane crashes, getting lost in bear-filled forests, and an iced over living room.

Reasons for Storytelling

The purpose of storytelling is generally to have a good time, but it also encourages proper speech, logical sequencing of events, and quick thinking. If you have entertaining children, you may never turn on the television set again. Older children can use storytelling to teach or to distract younger children. Maybe a little one is left behind while Mom and Dad go shopping. The attention of an older sister can make up for the hardship.

You can tape record your stories if you wish to preserve them for posterity or send them to relatives or friends as a gift. Most children can tell a story more easily than they can write one on paper. Memorable stories, whether historical or fictional, can become a resource for written projects later on. If your child insists that she doesn't have anything to write about, let her listen to her tape-recorded oral stories for inspiration.

What else can you do with storytelling? Your local library might appreciate a volunteer storyteller during the year. My children helped tell audience participation stories at our library. Each story included a repeated response from the audience. All the children made cat, bird, and dog sounds during a story about a pet show. The audience learned a short poem to repeat during a story about gophers. This project helped our local librarians, the audience enjoyed it, and it was an opportunity for my children to speak in public.

If your children really enjoy storytelling, they may want to enter local storytelling contests. Some children become professional entertainers at folk festivals after they have had hours of practice. Teens can work as guides at museums or zoos if they are skillful at public speaking. They might enjoy learning and telling real stories about the museum's artists or the zoo's animals as a summer or volunteer job.

In addition, many colleges now require business majors to take at least one speech class, and eventually your children will probably need to interview for jobs. Children need opportunities to present themselves coherently in front of an audience to build their skill and confidence for later in life. Story-telling can form the foundation for a college speech class, a job interview, and other necessary real-life presentations.

Project 6: Sing a Song

Singing is storytelling with a definite beat. Many children's stories have memorable rhythms. Rhythm is yet another form of communication. Some situations require original and memorable messages. Music is sometimes the best way to give a special gift to others, the best way to rejoice, or the best way to inspire others.

Give songs a try because working consciously with word patterns and rhythms will improve your child's oral and written communication. These are also essential parts of poetry, and some writers of prose add elements of poetry to their descriptions of scenery. They know that long uninspired descriptions can lose readers. Ellis Peters, author of *The Chronicles of Brother Cadfael,* and G. K. Chesterton, author of *The Father Brown Mysteries*, used striking rhythms and metaphors in their fiction stories.

Simple Songs for Everyday Situations

Of course, we aren't going to expect your child to produce a hit song, and your child may not like to sing at all. Some children are born composers and will surprise you if you give them the chance.

My younger daughter was complaining one day about having to make up her bed, so I told her to sing a work song until she finished. She sang something like "I've Been Working on the Railroad." Then I told her she could make up her own "Making the Bed" song. She did to my surprise, but unfortunately, I didn't write it down, so we don't remember it.

We had a Swimming song to sing on the way to the pool. When we lived farther away from Grandma, we had a Going to Grandma's House song. These songs added to our enjoyment of swimming and visiting Grandma. Not too long ago, they came up with a Taking Out the Trash song. It was rainy, and no one really wanted to take out the trash that day, but the job had to be done.

Resources:

This is how that song goes, and it's one of our better ones because it seems to make the job easier: "I like taking out the garbage, I like taking out the trash. Oh, I like taking out the garbage, I don't do it just for the cash!"

My children sometimes start with the music, and sometimes they begin with the words and work in the rhythm later. Songs based on chores seem to be the easiest for them to create.

Songs can be descriptive ("You Are My Sunshine"); tell a story ("Mary Had a Little Lamb"); list items ("The Twelve Days of Christmas"); share a message ("Let There Be Peace on Earth"); celebrate a holiday ("Hark the Herald Angels Sing"); and be silly, but fun to sing ("Ta Ra Ra Boom De Ay").

How Do You Start a Song?

It amazed me how long my children would work perfecting a parody. They spent hours rewriting "The Twelve Days of Christmas" with a science fiction theme, which was not my idea or their assignment for the day! They often work on projects together, each contributing something.

Simple re-writes might be the place to begin with songwriting. Perhaps, your children could take a short song, such as "Brother John" and change some words. For example, "Are you praying, are you praying, little child, little child, the noon bell is ringing, the noon bell is ringing, please come now, please come now." Praying could be changed to playing, running, or working.

"Mary Had a Little Lamb" could be sung as "Mary had a little son, little son, little son, Mary had a little son whose soul was white as snow."

How can your children transform "Row, Row, Row Your Boat", "Ten Little Indians", and "London Bridge"? Stick with simple folk tunes for young children.

What will you do with your songs? You can tape record them or write them down on paper. Use original songs in cards, letters, or stories. Write a special song to celebrate a special event, such as a family reunion or birthday. Perhaps your older children can write an educational song that will teach the younger ones the right way to tie their shoes or a chant to help them remember their address and phone number.

Project 7: Lists

List making is a simple form of writing. It's also a useful project for almost all ages. Teach your child how to stay organized, how to save money, how to study for tests, and how to keep important information available by using lists.

Young children can draw pictures, cut out pictures from magazines, copy words, or dictate to you to build a list. Instead of buying a poster that shows forms of transportation or community jobs, let your youngsters create their own visual list by searching for and cutting out pictures of these items. They can decorate their rooms with a collage of holy cards and printed biographies of saints.

Writers can add items to grocery lists, make up teaching aids for themselves or younger children, and write reminders to you about their various activities. You might want to invest in all sizes of notepads, chalkboards, memo boards, etc.

Some possibilities—

Grocery lists

Books I've Read

Books I Want to Read

Daily Mortifications for Lent

Virtues We Want to Develop

Family Petitions

The Forms of "To Be" in Latin

Chores

The Parts of the Mass

Homeschool Phone Numbers

Resources:

Developing Research and Organizational Skills

This is actually an on-going project in our family. It doesn't seem like much of a writing exercise, but the writer has to organize and sometimes research the information. List makers soon realize that inaccurate or incomplete information can cause trouble.

Do we need to buy canned tomatoes or fresh tomatoes? What is the area code for Joe Jones? (We have three area codes within our local calling range and must dial ten digits.) Who forgot to write eggs on the grocery list?

We usually set up permanent lists, such as chores and phone numbers on our computer, so the children are also working on their keyboarding skills.

DRAWING

3

Short Projects for Ready Writers

When Is Your Child Ready to Write?

Once your child has a few spelling words filed away in her memory, she's ready to put her talking down on paper with help and encouragement from Mom and Dad. This is the stage where I began to suggest punctuation, capitalizing, and other grammar rules. For some children, this stage occurs towards the end of first grade or during second grade or at about six and seven years of age. But if your child just isn't ready for writing more than a sentence or two, wait another six months.

Before teaching grammar rules, we memorized an audiotape called *Grammar Songs,* which introduced the parts of speech. Later, we progressed slowly rule by rule through Strunk and White's *The Elements of Style.*

If you are more comfortable using a formal grammar workbook to teach, take a hint from your child. Listen, and she will tell you by asking the right questions. If you have taught her some of the pre-writing skills, she should realize that the audience must be able to decipher her oral or written words. Children will begin to ask, "Is this right?" or "Can you read it?" They will look anxiously at your face for evidence of understanding or confusion.

Writing lists:

43

Writers first have to realize that someone else is going to read their work before they are ready to put effort into applying grammar rules.

If you haven't done so already, explain or remind your children that real writers are always concerned about their readers. Readers and writers will both be able to understand each other better if they follow the grammar rules. When you approach grammar from this perspective, you have an easy answer to the question, "Why do I have to learn all this?" "Because someone is going to read it!"

I've never heard a teen ask, "Why do I have to learn to drive?" They want to be able to drive, and they realize that they have to know the traffic laws. They want to receive their driver's license, and they don't want to get into an accident.

Communication is Worth the Work

"Why do I have to learn all this?" is actually a reasonable question. Sometimes it stems from a child's frustration. Maybe he isn't ready to handle the formal use of commas yet. Maybe he's being a bit lazy today. But maybe he doesn't yet realize the power of clear communication. In my work as an e-mail writer for a bank, we come across e-mails that we simply cannot understand even when several of us get together to try to decipher the meaning in an unpunctuated, misspelled message. Someone obviously wants us to do something with $50,000, but we aren't quite sure what. If we cannot make a reasonable guess, we have to write back requesting clarification or have someone call, both of which almost always annoy the customer.

If your child asks "Why do I have to learn this?", try to think of a time when she did not understand someone's communication either written or oral. Discuss the problems that occurred and the emotional conflict created because of the misunderstanding. Being understood and being able to understand others is a lifelong pursuit.

Communication is a significant skill. Being understood and being able to understand can make wonderful things happen between people. Yet too many "busy" projects kill that sense of significance. A child who can capture the attention of an audience with a story or a song knows that communication is worth the

work. A child who knows how to express herself so that others can understand her will have fewer problems with family, friends, and co-workers. Like learning to drive a car, learning to write, draw, and speak in public can take us places we want to go and help us avoid unnecessary accidents.

Ready for Informal Grammar

How do you begin grammar informally? Slowly and as the necessity arises is the least stressful for parent and child. Saying "This makes it easier to read," while making minor corrections in pencil is easier for children to handle than a lot of red marks on the thank you letter they have just labored over for half an hour.

Together write a list of a few basic grammar rules and post this near the writing area. Perhaps you add one new rule for each project, or work on one rule a week. Your child can practice grammar and proofreading by correcting his old writing projects if you saved copies. For example, take his "Books I Want to Read" list and proofread the titles of the books and author's names for capitalization. Review his old songs for punctuation.

We began with capitalizing all names and the first word of each sentence. You can review the pre-writing projects with capitalization in mind. Your child is already familiar with the projects and won't be faced with applying grammar rules and learning a new project at the same time. Let her know that you expect her to capitalize the names properly on the name tags she writes.

Appendix Four contains a list of simple grammar rules for beginning writers.

Project 8: Prayers

Writing prayers is a good beginning for children ready to write for several reasons. They have already been reciting prayers for a while and should be comfortable with the format. Prayers begin with simple salutations, such as "Dear God" or "Hail Mary," and they end with "Amen," so the writer knows exactly where to start and finish.

Prayers focus on something specific, such as the blessing of a meal or a special request. Beginning writers need that focus, so you will never tell them vaguely to "write a prayer." Tell them instead to write a prayer to bless the Thanksgiving meal.

Prayers can be fairly short, so they are not an overwhelming first project for a new writer. And they often are part of a family or community event, which makes them special. Children will understand that the prayer is not simply busywork but will be part of a ceremony. That's definitely motivating for any writer.

Children can be responsible for writing special prayers for many occasions, such as holy days, birthdays, secular holidays, and daily petitions. One reason for writing down daily petitions is to remember which ones and how many God has granted. We tend to forget these benefits.

The other day, a family member decided that her prayers were not being answered, and I had a ready list to prove to her that God was granting some of her petitions.

You may save special occasion prayers in a notebook or print them and keep them in a folder. Your children may want to decorate the front of the folder or notebook with paint, stickers, markers, fabric, felt, or magazine cut-outs. Perhaps you will want to set aside another notebook exclusively for daily petitions. Each family member can contribute, writing petitions on a daily or weekly basis. We never correct these petitions because God always understands what we mean even better than we do.

Project 9: Cyberpals

If you have access to email, perhaps your children can locate a cyberpal. My daughter wrote to a public school student one year and enjoyed it. She paid attention to her writing and spelling because her email style said a lot about her since they never met face to face.

She asked me to proofread her work and didn't complain about any corrections. She eagerly awaited each message and wrote more frequently than if she had had to wait for weeks to receive a regular letter.

Emails can be very short, and children won't have a piece of paper challenging them with its blankness. You won't need to hunt down a stamp to email a few sentences back and forth each week.

If you locate a regular pen-pal, you may be able to switch to email. Your local homeschool support group can potentially provide email pen-pals. That is probably the safest method of locating pen-pals for your children as you will know the parents already.

I'm very partial to pen-pals as I had an English pen-pal for years. We used so much paper and ink between us that we became a danger to the environment.

Chatrooms on the Internet

What about those open chat rooms on the Internet? Children's chat rooms can sometimes get chaotic, so I judge that I have to be there monitoring what's going on. The rooms get very full, and it's difficult for new writers to keep up with the flow of several different conversations. Use your own judgment.

See Appendix Two for web addresses for children.

Project 10: What's For Dinner?

You can't please everyone, but you can take written requests for meals. I often write menus and give my children each a day to plan. They write down what they want served, **and** they write down necessary ingredients after doing a little research in the refrigerator and pantry.

Eventually, children need to learn the importance of research, and this project works. They are very motivated to check on the amount of catsup left in the refrigerator if they want hotdogs Sunday afternoon. They are willing to suggest I buy brown sugar and more raisins for the oatmeal.

If you aren't used to writing full menus, then let your children write their meal requests the day before you shop as their writing assignment. Or set aside any day to write the meal requests, and include their list on your next shopping trip.

The sooner the meals appear on the table, the more reinforcement the activity generates, especially with younger children. They forget the connection between writing down "chili and pickles and rice" if the meal doesn't show up within a few days. This reinforcement is the evidence that communication is powerful and practical.

This is a fairly simple project that you can slip into a lesson plan. It also saves you time from meal planning. Your children will probably be thrilled to contribute written ideas. This is an excellent project for a child who normally does not enjoy writing. Most children do enjoy eating!

Project 11:
Card Occasions

Instead of spending $2-$4 on cards and missing a creative moment, design your own with personalized messages. Cards can be simple words written on colorful paper, use quotations, be humorous, or religious.

One year as a family project, we designed all our Christmas cards using card stock bought from a paper store and fabric paints. The paint stuck a bit to the envelopes, but everyone enjoyed them. We got lots of compliments.

Holidays, birthdays, get well soon, and many other occasions come up each month. Your family might decide to set aside a weekend twice a year to make cards ahead of time, or you can make each card as you need it. You will discover many opportunities for writing and sharing poetry, songs, congratulation speeches, and even very short stories for others. A winter poem would work well with a Christmas or New Year's card. A song about Grandma might be the right touch to a grandparents' day card.

Personalizing Cards

If your children don't know how to begin a birthday card to their Aunt Deb, talk to them about her interests. Well, Aunt Deb enjoys gardening and jumping on a trampoline.

Could we design a tall card showing the family jumping for joy? Each jumping person can contribute a word or two suitable for the occasion. Maybe we can draw flowers that spell her name on the front cover? On the inside we can re-write the Happy Birthday song or "How Does Your Garden Grow?"

What would cheer up a sick friend? Perhaps you could inflate a balloon and write on it a list of what you like best about your friend. Write a cheerful poem on brown or white postal paper and wrap a homemade cookie with the message.

Notes:

Give your children a few ideas or ask them questions to get them started. Encourage them to consider the interests and personality of the reader. This thoughtfulness helps focus and improve the communication. It's important in all kinds of writing, and the audience will appreciate it.

Supplies

Keep card stock and matching envelopes on hand along with art supplies. You can find them at major art and craft stores, but they are less expensive at office supply warehouses. We spent about $18 for over 125 sheets of cardstock and 50 envelopes. If you paid $2 each for 50 cards that's $100 and 50 lost writing projects. If you have the materials within reach, it's easier to sit down and create something immediately. This is also a great way to use up small amounts of paint, fabric, and other art materials.

Sometimes your children's old artwork can be transferred or transformed into unique cards if it is cut down to size or used as a collage. Glue scenes from old greeting cards and holy cards to card stock if your child isn't interested in drawing something new. You can even machine sew or hand-embroider cardstock with colorful threads.

Various computer software programs enable even young children to create professional looking cards. An American Greetings Spiritual card-making program costs about $20, if you are willing to pay the price of the program and learn how to use it.

Project 12:
Telephone Calls

Taking a Message

My children enjoyed answering the telephone at an early age. They never knew who might be trying to reach us, and of course, maybe the call was really for them. I enjoyed them answering the telephone, especially when my hands were sticky with dough or when I was out mowing the lawn. But occasionally, important messages from my husband, my parents, or in-laws didn't survive the memory transfer from child to mother. I would have dinner ready at six and then be upset that my husband didn't show up until eight although he had called—and left an oral message.

If your children want the privilege of using the telephone, teach them the responsibility of taking accurate telephone messages. At first, they can write down the name of the caller and the phone number, even if it's your neighbor whose number you have already memorized.

Obstacles to Message Taking

Taking a phone message may seem simple to an adult, but it actually involves several different steps. Don't expect your child to take a good message automatically.

To begin with, my children had a difficult time understanding people over the phone. They weren't hearing information clearly. Then they would get confused about who called. "Was it Aunt Jean or Aunt Jane?" And often they didn't write the phone number correctly. They had to learn to ask people to repeat vital information so they could double-check the message.

We practiced without the phone at the kitchen table first. I explained that the two most important pieces of information were the name of the caller and the caller's phone number. This is not obvious to some eight year olds. I dictated familiar names and numbers to them—Aunt Jane at 111-222-3333 and Grandma at 444-555-6666. They practiced writing these down quickly.

Then we called Dad. Dad's voice was familiar to them, so he gave them his phone number over the telephone so they could get used to holding the phone and writing at the same time. This is not an easy trick for an eight year old. It requires some manual dexterity and balancing. The children had to copy his number down and read it back to him. You can enlist the help of several relatives for this project. Keep pencils and paper near all telephones.

More Advanced Telephone Techniques

Later, children can take down additional information and learn to ask appropriate questions, such as, "How late may she return this call?" and "Do you want us to bring anything for the dinner?"

Older children can learn to give street directions to your house. Some adults have difficulty with this. We have a hand-drawn map posted near the phone with a list of directions.

You may want to teach your children to field sales calls also. They can respond with "She's not available to take your call now. Would you like to leave a message?" I am never available to take sales calls because I want to teach my children to think about purchases and not buy things on impulse or to donate money because of emotional appeals. However, I want them to treat salespeople politely.

Talking on the Telephone

When my shy younger daughter desperately wanted a pet rabbit, I suggested that she call pet stores to price equipment. She didn't want to talk to a stranger over the phone.

I then suggested she think through the questions first, writing them down and leaving space for answers. She hesitated a few days, but she really wanted that rabbit. She called and learned what items she needed for a rabbit and how much it would cost her. Her written script gave her confidence.

Then she wrote a new set of questions to ask a rabbit breeder, took a deep breath, and called several places. She finally found what she was looking for and named her new bunny Dominic. Later we had to change the name to Dominique, which is why we now have more rabbits.

Encourage your children to write down questions when they are seeking information over the phone from a stranger, a family member, or friend. At first, they will probably need help deciding what questions are important. Ask them "what information to do we want?" With practice, they will soon feel more confident and can write down the answers quickly so they don't forget the information they are given.

If they are calling a store, they should ask for product availability and store hours. If they are inviting Grandma for supper, they want to ask her what day and time is best for her and perhaps what she would like to eat. If they are asking a friend to join them in making sandwiches for a local charity, they also need to give accurate and relevant information—the date, time, what to wear, and that breakfast will be served.

This project also works well with long distance calls to relatives. Tell your children to write down the most important things they want to tell Grandpa before you make the call.

The privilege and responsibility of using the telephone can motivate your children to take accurate notes. They will learn to determine important facts and important gaps in their knowledge. Asking the right questions is a valuable skill.

Resources:

53

Project 13: Shared Story-Writing

One year we didn't want to send Easter cards, so we sent an Easter story. We did this project on the computer and used sound bites and graphics. Each family member contributed several paragraphs to the story. Our children were too young to write a whole story on their own, so we shared the writing.

We printed a copy of the finished story for some far away relatives, but our Easter visitors got the full effect when they came to visit. They sat down at our computer and were able to click on the icons for the sounds. We got requests for an encore. (This was in the days before any family members had internet access. Now we can email stories, photos, and songs to each other.)

Give yourself about a week or two to complete this project, especially if your children haven't learned how to add graphics or sound bites to their written work.

The story can be as long or short as you want. Gather everyone together and discuss appropriate plots. Remember, appendix one has a list of plot ideas.

You can divide the project by sentences, paragraphs, or characters. Perhaps you can have one child responsible for writing as others dictate, choose one to act as proofreader, and let one contribute dialogue. Even very young children can contribute ideas or names of characters. Often my children included themselves in the story as the main characters.

Besides learning teamwork, shared storytelling is the easiest way to get a child to begin writing longer items. They should be comfortable with oral storytelling, but they still may need help with writing a whole story. It may seem an impossible task because one story involves plots, characters, description, a title, and dialogue. Divide the various aspects of story writing among your children.

My children enjoyed this activity so much that they still talk about it. If your children enjoy it, it might be a good project during your Christmas holidays or summer vacation. Perhaps

they could write a story for New Year's Day about making resolutions, or a story about Independence Day with their pet as the main character. We often celebrated holidays, such as St. Valentine's Day, by writing and then sharing our own stories.

Preserve Your Stories

These stories are definitely "keepers." You will want to save copies even if you give the original to friends and family. Keep your creations well organized in a notebook, folder, or on a computer disk. If you write Easter stories each year, you can make a ritual of re-reading all your Easter stories annually. These stories will show your child's progress through the years.

Resources:

Project 14: Family Newsletter

Mail seasonal newsletters to friends and relatives with help from your children. The year we didn't create our own Christmas cards, we wrote a family newsletter. We had also just moved, and we wanted to announce our new address in a memorable way.

Each child had his own column—Anthony's Angle, Betsy's Banter, and Cathy's Corner. They explained what they had been busy doing in the past few months in their own words. They could write as much or as little as they chose.

I also write a yearly family reunion newsletter for my father's side of the family. My children have an opportunity to organize and edit the family news that people send in at the beginning of each year. Thus they will take Aunt Jean's notes about her business trips and write a paragraph. They also add clip art to the newsletter. Children can write or print address labels, fold and staple the letters, and drop them in the mailbox.

You don't have to have a computer to write your own newsletter, but it certainly helps. You can type or neatly write the information and then photocopy the pages, but realize that that will probably take longer than a week or two. If you don't have a computer, draw a mock-up of the layout page by page, estimating how much space you will need and where artwork will go. Use original poems, songs, drawings, and Scripture verses as fillers. No white, that is, empty space, is allowed except for page margins.

Columns make a newsletter more official looking, but they are more difficult to handle if you don't have a computer. Study your local newspaper or newsletters that you receive to find a style you like.

If you have an older writer with more experience, he could tackle the job by himself. He can interview family members to gather the data and write a short newsletter. Set aside about 2-4 weeks, depending upon the ability of your child, but do set a deadline.

Seasonal newsletters are ways to publish your children's small pieces of writing, such as poems, lists, and short stories, but it also provides them the opportunity to write facts creatively. Facts don't have to be boring. They can be presented in interesting ways. A birth announcement can include a cartoon or be done in an interview format. Your children could write a poem to notify people of your change of address. They could simply write "Guess who moved?" and create a border using self adhesive address labels (with your new address!) around the edges of the question. Nonfiction writing can also be very creative writing.

Resources:

Notes:

Project 15: Cartooning

We have not yet tackled this project. It's still a legible line on our "To Do" list, although we have discussed possible subjects.

A cartoon doesn't have to be humorous, but where do you begin? Why not start with a favorite family saying or a child's hobby?

My husband was looking at my Miraculous Medal one day, and I pointed to his and said, "We match; we must be married." He replied, "Yes, we're Mary'ed all right." As one of our frequently used family puns, we need to get it in print. Preserve your favorite family saying or pun in a framed cartoon hung on your wall.

A local chiropractor has a framed cartoon of himself and an anonymous patient in his office. I used a cartoon of my sister and her pet birds for a "bird day" card.

My cousin was telling me about her eighteen month old son talcum powdering her while she took a nap on the couch. She woke up covered in white. I put the story in the family newsletter, but it could easily have been turned into a memorable cartoon.

You might want to make a whole book of family cartoons. Consider interesting statements from your children, such as "Mom, look at the sunset God painted!" or "If you move to a new house when I'm grown up, will you tell me how to get there?" These are wonderful to share in later years at family gatherings when your children and you may have forgotten about these childhood views and questions.

Cartoons relieve stress and frustration, too. If your child is bogged down in a math lesson, have him take a five minute break and draw a cartoon face about how he feels at the moment. He will hopefully end up laughing, and the short break will give him renewed energy to continue with the lesson. Cartoons can help us control our emotional moments and give us a new perspective. Cartoon breaks won't be wasted time if parents and children use them wisely.

What if Your Child Isn't an Artist?

Don't skip this project even if your children aren't artists. They can use stick figures or roly-poly circle people.

Thumbprint characters are easy for children to create. Simply press your thumb into ink (any color but black) and then onto paper. Add eyes, mouth, arms, and legs with a black felt tip pen.

Use ready-made stickers of people and animals to create cartoons. See what you can create with computer clip art, or create posed photographs to illustrate your ideas.

Resources:

Project 16: Important Notes to Others

Occasionally, you will find opportunities for your child to leave personal notes or reminders for yourself or others. For example, if I think we may not return from a field trip before my husband gets home from work, we might leave him a note to remind him of our trip and at what hour we plan to return, that his supper is in the refrigerator, and would he please put the clothes that are in the washing machine into the dryer.

We want our children to get into the courteous habit of communicating important information to others. This is primarily to instill politeness, but these little notes also provide useful writing practice. I suppose we could tape the messages on a tape recorder and leave that in the middle of the table, but creativity is not really the point of this project. It's more efficient to jot down a brief note.

We also write notes to people outside the family. Our children own several pets, which need care when we leave for a vacation. They are responsible for leaving proper instructions with the pet sitter. If your child needs to leave a pet in someone's care, have her write a list of instructions and other useful information. For example, your neighbor or pet sitter needs to know how much food, water, and perhaps medicine your pet usually needs, and even what a pet's favorite toy or game is. Leave the vet's name and number and where you can be reached in an emergency.

Another prime opportunity for writing is asking a favor. Your child might want you to run an errand for him when you drive into town. Ask him to write down exactly what he wants you to do. "Please drop off my letter to my pen-pal at the post office." "Please buy AAA batteries and a light bulb for my science project." This has kept me from buzzing about town on various errands and then returning home to a disappointed child. Who knows why we forget these important things, but I know I do—unless it's written down.

Your child might want you to ask the choir director questions about an up-coming event. Have him write down the questions about proper dress, time, and location. Maybe he wants his sister to do a chore for him while he is out of town. If he writes down these favors, someone will be more likely to remember and do them.

Perhaps more importantly, your child is not neglecting the responsibility for his pets, chores, or personal activities. The chance of miscommunication is lessened, and he will begin to understand that he must plan ahead to handle his responsibilities. Although he may be excited about going on a camping trip with his buddy, his fish still need attention, and he needs to make arrangements to have the trash taken out on trash day.

Instilling Responsibility Through Communication

You may have noticed that we require our children to handle a lot of situations regarding their personal interests, such as pets and activities. Many of our writing projects arise from their everyday experiences.

We have expected them to be responsible if they want to have their own pet and if they want to participate in the choir. If your children are not used to handling these situations, please build up their level of responsibility slowly.

One teen actually ended up in jail because her mother suddenly decided to stop taking charge of her daughter's affairs. The daughter—who was a new driver—received a ticket for a minor traffic violation. Her mother took the ticket, telling the daughter that she would handle it and not to worry about it, and then never paid the fine. Instead, she was waiting and hoping that her daughter would ask her for the ticket and handle it herself.

Someone else in authority was keeping tabs on that ticket, and so some months later, the daughter was arrested. My husband had time to reflect on responsibility while driving the father to the police station late that evening. That experience motivated us to give our children more responsibility.

Resources:

61

Notes:

Obviously, some situations are too difficult for children to handle without your help. I try to stand by during telephone calls and personal encounters. For example, my daughter called a bookstore about a defective book she had recently purchased. She had read to about chapter twenty and discovered that the next chapter was not twenty-one but chapter nineteen all over again.

This store was a long drive away, so I asked her to call ahead to explain the situation and ask the store to reserve another book for her. I didn't want to make the long drive to discover that the store was temporarily out of stock or that all their copies of that book were defective. The clerk was not helpful for some reason. In this situation, we neglected to write down the instructions to give the clerk, which caused my daughter some confusion and embarrassment.

I'm ready to step in if I think an adult is being condescending, or if my child is getting confused about the situation. In the case of the unhelpful clerk, he could have been unsure as to what she was trying to communicate, and he could have been busy with a line of customers. It might have helped him to have our instructions better prepared and in writing. I know it would have helped my daughter to have a script in her hands. We both learned our lesson with that experience.

Project 17: Pros and Cons

The basic requirement for this project is a decision or a problem. Writing down facts and possible solutions to our problems focuses our attention. Writing puts our thoughts into specific words that we can read and reflect on.

Many words are signposts or symbols that lead us in particular directions. The phrase "Home, Sweet Home" brings a rush of memories. The word "home" leads our minds to a particular place among particular people. When you are trying to solve a problem, a word signpost helps you focus.

Four Step Problem Solving

If you have no decisions or problems, you will have to move along to the next project. Otherwise, get out pencil and paper. I will explain the four steps in detail after listing them.

1. Write down the problem.

2. List possible solutions.

3. Mentally test each solution by listing the pros and cons of each.

4. Choose the best answer to the problem.

Writing the Problem

If we have only a vague idea of what the decision or problem is, then we often have difficulty figuring out a solution. Sometimes, in writing down a problem clearly, you will begin to see solutions. Specific words will help focus your thinking. The real problem might be that you don't understand what the problem is.

A child might think that the problem is that "Math is too hard". Encourage him to restate the problem in a new way. Ask for specifics about what part of math is hard—counting, adding, borrowing, decimals? "I don't understand percent problems" will

lead your child in a particular direction. "I'm afraid that I'm not going to do as well as my sister did" could mean the problem has little to do with math.

Teach your child to reflect on the written problem and to locate the words that act as signposts before listing solutions. The signposts in the above problem statements are "understand", "percent problems", and "afraid".

Listing Solutions

List possible solutions that are related to the clearly stated problem. This is also the questioning stage. Ask how, when, why, and where. How can I solve this problem? When do I need to solve the problem—immediately or over a lifetime? Why is this problem or decision so important? Where do I need to go for support or more information? These questions can suggest solutions. For instance, if you have limited time to solve the problem, you don't want to waste time thinking of complicated solutions you can't use. Perhaps you begin to see that you need more information before coming up with solutions. Perhaps the problem isn't even as important as you thought it might be.

Writing the Pros and Cons

It can be difficult to predict the consequences of some actions, but most of us can make reasonable guesses about the future.

For example, our family artist wasn't sure what to create for an art contest. We listed three possibilities—a drawing of a Rosary with family scenes representing each large bead, a sculpture of our family at Mass, and a sculpture of the artist's bedroom. We guessed the Rosary was going to be an obvious choice for most participants. She wanted something unique. If she sculpted the whole family, she guessed that she wouldn't have time to complete the project. The bedroom was the best choice because it matched the theme of the contest, she had easy access to it while working, and we predicted that no one else would think of the idea. She picked a winner.

The Solution

Finally, choose the best answer. Sometimes this will be obvious as in the case of the art contest. Other times, it will be difficult. Then you will want to take more time to review your solutions and their advantages and disadvantages. Prayer always helps, too.

This method helped us decide which house to buy a few years ago. We wanted to move from a rent house that was falling apart on us and creating health problems. The new house needed to have a stove that worked, a strong fence to keep our dog in the yard, and hard floors to alleviate my husband's allergy problems. We also had heard a rumor that the owners would be moving soon from Hong Kong, and we figured we had about six months to make a decision.

Our resources included a real estate agent, a map of the city, the Internet, and the newspaper. We knew what we were looking for, and we had a set price range. Advantages and disadvantages arose. Was a swimming pool a pro or a con? We decided it was a con. Was a two story house acceptable? How much yard did we want?

Finally we had to choose between two houses. We drew up a new list based on these houses. Each member of the family had a chance to state his opinion. After writing everything down, we marked our consensus of the most important pros and cons. Both of the houses were equal according to the issues we originally stated. So we eventually based our choice on secondary issues.

Thinking on Paper

Thinking on paper not only helps children and adults with prudent decision making, but it's good practice for note taking and research. The writer often has to sift through ideas and information to select what is relevant. He has to choose key words that are related to his subject.

Our lives are full of decisions—what to cook for Easter dinner, where to go for vacation, what shrubs to plant in the southern flowerbeds, whether or not to buy a trampoline.

Resources:

Not every decision will be as major as buying a house, and not every decision will be worth writing down. Take advantage of those times your child comes to you with a problem that looks like it needs clarifying.

Notes:

4

Advanced Projects for Real Writers

The following projects require spelling and grammar skills, but they also require planning, thought, and some technical skills. Writers, your audience is going to expect more from you now that you have some life and academic experience.

You will frequently be writing and speaking to a wider and more adult audience. Therefore, you need to consider the requirements of the audience before beginning.

What will interest your audience? What format does the audience prefer? For example, if you want to send a letter to your aunt who has bad eyesight, use large print as a courtesy. If you are designing a teaching aid for a young child, use simple words and pictures.

You can and should do many of these projects with little or no supervision from your parents. Please discuss the projects with your parents and get their approval. Your parents may think of new ideas or particular situations to help you get started, but try to do as much research, writing, and proofreading on your own as you reasonably can.

Project 18: Wearable Words

A pithy comment may take a long time to write, but if you have an important message to share, you can wear it. What would you like to say to the general public? Do you want to make people smile? Would you like to make someone stop and ponder a great truth? Would you like to share your faith?

If you have received the sacrament of Confirmation, you can bear witness to Catholic ideals by wearing your faith on your sleeve or shirt front. It can be a healthy alternative to some t-shirts and slogans you may have seen around your town.

My children would sometimes ask why people wore rude t-shirts, meaning shirts that had ugly pictures or words. I replied that the people were promoting those ideas, but I added that we could wear polite t-shirts to make up for the rude ones, even if we had to make them ourselves.

What will you write on your t-shirt before you put it on? Express your belief in homeschooling, in God, in the family. You can spread devotion to the Sacred Heart of Jesus, to the Rosary, and to your favorite saint.

What would you like to share with the world? An Easter message? Ten Important Reasons to Homeschool? A great quotation by G. K. Chesterton?

Maybe a real situation can inspire you. One friend becomes annoyed when she drives past a particular church. It sometimes promotes a brief anti-Catholic message on an outdoor sign. I use these to teach apologetics lessons to my children. We check for new messages every time we pass by. Could you debate the message "Faith Alone, Bible Alone, and Grace Alone?" which was their message for February, 1999 with a solid statement?

Supplies and Options

How many different ways can you wear your words? Create your own bumper stickers, book covers, handkerchiefs, t-shirts, caps, jackets, and tote bags. Office supply warehouses have sticker paper that you can cut down to size for designing your own bumper stickers. Arts and crafts stores will have t-shirts, caps, tote bags, aprons, and many other items you can decorate.

You have several options for creating wearable words. Special computer software like Hanes T-Shirt Maker allows you to design your own iron-on transfers. (Unfortunately, these don't hold up to washing very well.)

If you aren't using a software program, then begin with scratch paper cut to approximately the length and width of the space you want to fill. Try to come up with about three different designs. Move the artwork (if any) and the lettering around. Try different styles of lettering and different words until you are satisfied with the result.

Once you like the design, you can order a quantity of t-shirts or tote bags printed with your message from screen printing companies. Iron on your statement with a letter kit, or paint it with fabric paints. Maybe you could machine stitch your message on fabric.

Brevity, Clarity, and Neatness Count

Your message has to be short and clear. Every word must be vital because space is limited, and you don't want your lettering to be too small to be read. You don't necessarily have to write complete sentences. For example, adorn your book bag with "St. Francis de Sales, Patron Saint of Writers". Your bumper sticker might read "Hurray for homeschool." Design a T-shirt with a hand painted Rosary and the caption "Have you called her blessed?"

If you want your readers to remember your message, remember that you must present it clearly and neatly. A poor presentation can destroy your credibility.

Resources:

Project 19: Study Guides

Study guides are lists that lead you through a subject toward a goal. You've probably written lists before, but a study guide is usually more formal than something like a grocery list.

If you plan to homeschool your own children someday, you will want to be able to write and maintain study guides for their educational benefit. Many states require parents to have a written curriculum. A curriculum is actually a collection of study guides. It indicates what subjects, resources, and goals teachers have planned for students.

A Real Life Example

I like to give my children an opportunity each year to study a subject on their own. They choose something they are interested in learning. It might be map-making, harmonica lessons, woodworking, or sculpture. I want them to discover that they can learn various activities and ideas on their own. They can continue learning throughout their lives, especially in subjects that deeply interest them.

They must have a definite goal in mind, locate resources, and keep to a budget. Otherwise, they tend to drift around in a subject without any clear idea of what they are doing and why.

For instance, by the end of the semester, they should present a collection of finished maps, entertain us with several harmonica selections, or have completed a carpentry project. Each subject will have its own particular process, necessary resources, and goal.

Parental Permission

If you have a deep interest in learning something new, first get your parent's permission. If they don't approve of your suggested subject, you won't need to bother writing a study guide.

However, some parents might want to see how much thought you have given to an idea. If you respectfully and thoughtfully present them with a guide of how you will apply yourself to the intricacies of landscape design, they might be impressed enough to allow you to plant a few shrubs and put in a fish pond.

Once you get the go ahead, ask yourself a few questions before writing. Why does the topic appeal to me? What resources will I use? Do I need to consider cost? How much time do I have available?

How to Develop Your Study Guide

Let's walk through the creation of a study guide. We'll say that you are interested in designing a Web page or Web log (a blog) for homeschooled teens. At the top of a sheet of paper, write "Study Guide: Learning to Design a Web Page/Log." I am assuming that you have never designed a Web page or blog. Therefore, this is the subject you need to learn about before you can design it.

Your goal is "to let people know what homeschooling is like from a young adult's perspective" or whatever your goal is. Write it down. Your goal keeps you focused and determines where to start and when to stop your design project. If your goal is too broad, you won't be able to cover the subject adequately. We are finite people with finite amounts of time in which to accomplish our goals, so make your goal specific.

Naturally, you are experienced at being homeschooled, but maybe you don't know how to use the software for Web pages and blogs. So how do you proceed from subject to goal to page or blog? You must locate the necessary resources.

You head for the library and discover twenty books on Web pages. You log onto the Web and find link after link of information on blogs. This is why you need a study guide. It reminds you that you aren't going for a Ph.D. in Web mastering. Remember, you want to design one Web page or Web log for and about homeschooled teens before you reach twenty.

You decide that your strategy will be to choose a software program, such as FrontPage for a Web page, and learn to use the main features to design your own page. Is that the best starting point? Well, maybe you should do that after you look at examples

of Web pages and get an idea of how to put one together. So first, you search the Web for design ideas. Be sure to write down the links on your study guide and determine what you like or don't like about each design. Then when you begin to learn FrontPage, you have an idea of what features you need to learn to create your own site.

If you want to create a Web log, the process is similar. First, visit some blogs and find out how people design and use the blogs. Write down the links and any ideas that you can use. Then head over to www.blogger.com to take the tour and register for the free blog software. Be sure to read the Terms of Service and perhaps discuss with your parents. You may want to take notes as you work through the process of learning how to edit and publish your posts and photos. Although a blog is generally an on-going journal, you may decide to limit yours to one week or one semester unless you get so involved that you want to continue writing.

When you begin applying your newfound knowledge by creating the Web page or Web log, you may discover that you need to go back to your resources or gather more resources to accomplish your goal. Remember that you are writing a guide not a legal document that has to be followed to the letter. You can change your study guide.

When you create a Web page or blog, also remember that this information is accessible to millions of people. Practice prudence and keep your private identifying information, such as your name and residence, off the Web.

By the time you have reached your goal of designing a Web page or Web log, you should have a complete study guide. In fact, someone else should be able to take your study guide and follow it from subject to Web page or log, reviewing your progress. You have left a solid paper trail similar to a scientist recording experiments.

A Different Kind of Study Guide

What you actually did in the hypothetical case above was to build a study guide as you learned the subject. You were writing and testing it as you went.

If you already know a subject and want to teach it to someone else, you follow a slightly different path in producing your study guide. But both kinds of study guides keep you focused on your goals.

1. Consider your audience. How much of the subject should you teach? What do they need to know and why? State the subject and goal.

2. What are the time limits to achieve the goal?

3. What are the best resources that you are familiar with? Will these satisfy the goal? Do you need to create or find better resources?

4. How will you use these resources? Will your students read and answer questions? Discuss and experiment?

5. How will you know when your students have reached the goal? Will they present a project, an oral report, or need to pass a written test?

You may not know all of the answers, but you will have a better idea of how to use your resources of time, money, and effort if you can write and apply practical study guides.

Resources:

Project 20: Writing Your Own Tests

This project definitely requires approval from your parents. Once you gain some experience, you can prepare tests for younger children, and if you plan to homeschool your own children, you will want this kind of experience now while your parents can evaluate your work.

You might want your parents to read the next four paragraphs if they are skeptical about the idea. It's a risky concept since you have no one to blame if you fail your own test!

Why Bother?

Why would you or your parents want you to write your own test? By thinking like a test maker instead of a test taker, your perspective changes. It's a new way of looking at information, a new way of thinking and writing. Instead of reading your history and wondering vaguely what questions will be on the test, read your history and develop good questions. Write them down.

Actually writing clear questions is difficult. It can be more difficult than writing the answers. But I find that I learn more when I ask questions instead of passively waiting to be questioned. In fact, a long time ago, an interviewer was so impressed with my questions that he wanted to hire me for a job. But I realized from my questions and his responses that I didn't want that job.

Learning and writing often involve thoughtful questioning and listening. My sister used to be ridiculed because as a technical writer for a computer company, she asked many, many questions of the computer experts. Someone suggested that she would be fired for being so ignorant. Instead she was promoted! Her writing was more technically correct than the others precisely because she dared to ask questions.

When you are working at a job whether at home or in a business, you will not always be "tested" for a passing grade. Your job performance at draining the hot water heater or conducting a survey will be your responsibility. You may receive on-the-job training, seminars, or demonstrations as technology and business methods change over the years. So you must learn to ask good questions and write down or remember the answers.

How Do You Write a Test?

Once you have studied the material, choose the key facts and write your questions. Will you have true-false statements, fill in the blanks, multiple choice, or essay questions? Can you write thoughtful questions? Evaluate your own work.

When you are ready, give your test to your parents to evaluate. Ask if you covered the key ideas. Ask if the questions are clear. A day or two later, they can give you your own test to take. You have no excuses for not earning a passing grade on this one.

If your parents permit you to write a test for younger children, consider your audience, and don't assume that you know the information. You must test them on the material appropriate for their level not yours. Review their lessons. Can you write questions that they can understand? How do you know if a test is too hard or too easy? How long does a test have to be to adequately examine the knowledge of the test taker?

A Variation on the Test Theme

I also have given my children a test that had the answers. Their task was to write appropriate questions. If your parents just do not like the idea of you writing your own test, try this variation. It will almost certainly be a time saver for your mother to write down one or two word answers and then leave a long blank for you to write appropriate questions, but it may take longer for her to grade, so double it as a writing project and a science or history lesson.

This is an easier test than an essay exam, but much harder than fill in the blank or multiple choice. You will be practicing writing questions and testing your academic knowledge at the same time.

As an example, for science, I would write "oxygen", expecting my children to write a question like "What is a gas that we breathe?" or "What do plants give off after taking in carbon

dioxide?" If they just wrote, "What is the name of a gas?" they didn't get much credit.

For history, I might write "Joan of Arc". Some possible questions would be "Who was first called a heretic and later named a saint?" and "Who raised the siege of Orleans in the Hundred Years War?"

Project 21: Journals with a Theme

People write journals for different reasons. A mother might write one during her pregnancy as a gift to her child. Gardeners often keep careful records of their successes and failures with various plants and locations. Runners write down notes about their workouts in order to prevent over-training and to maintain their peak performance.

We have discovered that writing a journal with a specific theme is more interesting than jotting down daily events. Select a subject of interest and keep your journal focused on the subject. Here is a list of ideas:

Scriptural or homily meditations

Favorite sports you are involved in

Recipes you develop or find

Bird watching

Summaries of books you enjoyed reading

Art and craft ideas

Field trips you've taken

Annual events you volunteer for with names of contacts, appropriate clothing, and operating ideas

Record of spiritual progress

Mistakes you don't ever want to make again

As an example, I have several notebooks of information about many library books I have read. If I want to re-read a book, use a book as a reference, or recommend a book to a friend, I can flip through my notebooks and locate the library call number, author, date of publication, or a summary of the contents. I only keep records for books I don't already own. This keeps me from spending the family food budget on books I think I really have to have for future reference.

Project 22: Magazine & Newsletter Submissions

Do you have knowledge, a craft idea, an entertaining story, or a poem that you would like to share with others? Who would be interested in your information or story?

Depending upon your age and the subject, you can send your story or poem to children's magazines. Look at children's magazines at home and in your library. Read what others have contributed to determine if your writing fits the same general tone and age group. Most publications have a specific audience and theme.

If you belong to a special interest group, such as 4-H, Scouts, Little Flowers, or Tarcisians, your group may have a magazine or newsletter that would welcome submissions from members. Perhaps you could write an article for your homeschooling newsletter. Call the editor and ask if he is looking for articles on anything specific.

The Writer's Market

Your local library probably has a reference book called the *Writer's Market*. This book, which is updated yearly, lists publishers and magazines under many categories with information on submissions. Some publishers prefer to work with previously published writers or literary agents only. You have a better chance if you submit to editors who are willing to work with new writers and accept a lot of free-lance materials.

Free-lance writers, as opposed to salaried writers, don't work exclusively for one publisher or company. They usually write for various publications on speculation. Speculation means that you write without any guarantee of being paid for the writing. No one has authorized you to write the article, but that doesn't mean that an editor wouldn't be interested in your information.

When you write for national publications, many have specific submission guidelines. Some editors want photos or sketches

included. They may want to know if you have published anything previously. Generally, editors want to see double-spaced pages, and your name, page number, and title at the top of each page. Write a cover page if the item is longer than two pages. The cover page has the title, your name, address, phone number, and email address if you have one.

Keep in mind that editors often have a lot of submissions from which to choose. Your writing may not get published, but by submitting your work and studying published articles, you will learn more about writing well. If you receive a rejection slip from a publication, it doesn't necessarily mean that you aren't becoming a good writer. Some well-known authors papered their walls with rejection slips before breaking into print.

Resources:

Notes:

Project 23: Proofreading Skills

Proofreading is a necessary skill for serious writers. By proofreading others' work, you will learn to read your own work more objectively.

If you have younger brothers or sisters, your mother might appreciate your proofreading their work. You want to find mistakes that they shouldn't be making, but be gentle. Encourage them to write well. Try to make suggestions instead of telling them what they did wrong.

For example, you read the following sentence in your sister's letter to Grandma: "my nu dog is small and wite." Suggest that Grandma will have an easier time reading the letter if the "m" is capitalized. Grandma will expect to see the first word of each sentence capitalized. Grandma might not understand the words "nu" and "wite" because the correct spelling is "new" and "white."

Grandma can probably handle one long paragraph that should technically be separated into three or four. A few skipped commas are okay if your sister has not learned much about commas yet. She may dangle a participle or two, but remember that she can't write above her conversational level. Grandma won't expect her to talk or write like an adult.

Your mother or father might want you to proofread their letters or other writing for mistakes. Your goal as a proofreader is not necessarily limited to finding mistakes, but to cooperate with the writer to produce writing that is easily understood and accurate.

Proofreading Marks

I sometimes use proofreading marks on my own work, and you can learn a few, but they won't help if the author doesn't understand them.

To delete a word, draw a single horizontal line through it. To delete a letter, draw a vertical line. The abbreviation "sp." means to spell out the circled word or to correct the spelling.

The paragraph mark, ¶, indicates where a paragraph should begin. The letters "u.c." means upper case, or capitalize. And therefore, "l.c." is used for lower case, or do not capitalize. Use a ^ symbol to indicate where to insert letters, words, or punctuation marks.

Proofreading is more complicated than the simple versions I have suggested, but simple proofreading is within your ability. It should be part of the writing process. It's useful for both writers and readers to prevent possible miscommunication. Few people write a perfect letter, article, or poem with no mistakes in the first draft.

Resources:

Project 24: Instructional Aids

An instructional or educational aid can be almost anything as long as it is used to help someone learn something. A bit of string can be an instructional aid if you use it to demonstrate how to tie a square knot.

If you are interested in homeschooling your children, you will want to know how to write or design instructional aids. You can also develop instructional aids to help yourself with your own studies now and later on if you enter college or another school.

A friend sold her used college books for the price of new books. How did she accomplish that? She took good notes and sold her notebook (an instructional aid) along with the book. She said she had no problem reselling her books, and her clear well-organized notes helped her earn top grades.

Learning is Going On All Around You

Can you write educational aids for others? Learners are all around you, including people you see frequently. Maybe your brother needs help with history. Together you could create a timeline or chart of names. Perhaps a friend is teaching a religious class to third grade children and would like help designing a poster about the parish's patron saint. A song or poem can be an instructional aid. For example, St. Thomas Aquinas wrote poetry about the Eucharist, which you could share with a religious class. How could you present his key ideas in a memorable way?

Public Instructional Displays

Your local library might be open to you setting up an instructional display for the benefit of the public. An instructional display is a collection of several instructional aids. If you are interested in music, you could choose various biographies of musicians and include albums or CDs of some of their famous works to display. Just make sure that you do not indicate that Mozart composed Beethoven's Fifth Symphony by an awkward placement of the biographies and music. Proofread your work. Is the information correct? Could it be misinterpreted?

My children enjoy looking at these displays when entering and leaving the library. These displays can be inspiring and educational. They will definitely be public.

Sharing Your Interests with Your Community

My son and younger daughter volunteered to teach other children about rabbit care when they saw a notice asking for help with the children's summer reading programs. They made notes of topics they wanted to discuss and took the rabbits along for display. The children in the audience were allowed to pet them at the end of the program.

When they were standing up to share their rabbit knowledge, they were glad to have their notes or the rabbits to hold onto. Instructional aids can give a nervous teacher enough extra confidence to face a group of strangers. This was also a great opportunity for my children to practice public speaking in a low-key group.

Our city's parks and recreation department regularly asks for people to share new ideas. An eighteen year old high school graduate taught several art classes for the summer of 1999. She had to write an explanation of the classes and submit these for the registration brochure.

Strive for Neatness, Organization, and Brevity

Charts, lists, and diagrams are useful for many people trying to learn new material. The material may seem simple to you, but it probably isn't for your audience. If you organize material into small chunks, you often make it memorable, or at least, easy to follow. For example, if you want to teach someone how to make a dried apple wreath, you can list the necessary craft supplies and then the step by step process.

If you want to teach children how to use sign language for signing songs, you could use diagrams. Make sure your

Resources:

educational material is well-organized and neat whether it is a list, a timeline, or a set of instructions. Proofread it to make sure that every word counts.

Notes:

Project 25: Memory Book

If you are starting a new undertaking, or if you have lots of loose family photos, consider making a memory or scrapbook. This could be a memory book for you to chart your progress while you are earning a black belt in martial arts, an album of a family vacation, or anything of interest to you.

You will be creating a wonderful time capsule to share with others later in life, such as your future spouse, children, and grandchildren. Look through these special books on days when you think that nothing is going right in the world. At the very least, your photos and memorabilia won't be dispersed all over the house, and you will exercise your creative and organizational skills.

If you decide to teach a class from Project 24, you can compile a book of the instructional aids, your evaluation of the class, notes or comments you received from your students, and so forth. This kind of a memory book will help you improve your next class.

Pull the Pieces Together

Gather and organize the material first. You can organize it chronologically or topically. For instance, your family vacation can begin with packing the car and end with unpacking the car. Other family photos could be separated into birthday parties, family pet photos, and relatives without regard to the time the pictures were photographed.

You can purchase inexpensive albums from discount and office supply stores. As an art project, you can make your own album or decorate a plain inexpensive album with fabric, wrapping paper, road maps, or felt.

Notes:

Add Words to the Pictures

Once your material is organized, write captions and headings if appropriate. Perhaps you can include written personal reminiscences or opinions.

After a wonderful trip to New Orleans, we put together a vacation album of our trip. I wanted to remember some areas where we were not allowed to take photos, so I left the picture space blank and wrote captions describing what we weren't allowed to photograph. Thus, a caption under one blank says, "Dining Room at Oak Alley Plantation—note the flycatchers on the table."

Handling Mementos Other Than Photos and Papers

If you have items that won't fit in an album, make a memory box or memory folder. Decorate the box or folder as an art project. Tag bulky items with captions or paragraphs that will aid your memory of the event. Blank stickers are useful for labeling items you can't or don't want to write on. If the sticker isn't large enough for the necessary information, use string and card stock to make up labels. For example, if you want to tag a baby shoe, you could attach a sticker to the sole of the shoe or tie a card onto the shoelaces to identify the wearer.

We kept our identifying numbers from local fun-runs in a special folder. On the back of our number, we wrote the event, the day, and our time. The weather and the organization of the event were important information, too. If brochures were available, we added those. From year to year, we could decide if we wanted to re-enter the Dino-Dash or the Terry Fox Fun Run and determine if our times were improving—or not.

Project 26: Family History

Are you interested in genealogy? I began my children's introduction to history with family stories. They could relate familiar faces to events and places. History became something they could see, hear, feel, and even smell and taste. My mother bakes Christmas cookies each year using my father's mother's recipe brought from the old country.

If I didn't know any family history, I wouldn't have been able to introduce my children to the "living" past. The Christmas cookies would not have extra meaning for them. Remember, too, that family history is a good resource for storytelling.

Research Resources

This is probably a long-term project depending on how far back you want to research. Resources abound, so be prepared to sharpen your research and question asking abilities. The Internet has websites for family history. See Appendix Two for web addresses. You can check church records, interview family members, and sort through old newspapers and family possessions when beginning your search.

Beware of some companies who would appreciate you buying their generic family histories. These are often expensive and add little of real value to your research. As my husband said, "Everyone couldn't have a coat of arms. Somebody had to play the part of peasants."

It might seem easier to let someone else do the work for you when you run into dead ends. Think of it as a treasure hunt. Sometimes you will turn up rocks, but you also will find at least a gold nugget or two, especially if you pay attention and ask thoughtful questions.

Notes:

Gather Your Data in Various Forms

Be prepared to take many notes. You may want to draw pictures, take photographs, or locate maps. Don't worry about collecting more information than you can use. Get as much as possible at first. Sift through it later for the gold nuggets.

In the end, you will have to decide how to present the material to other family members. Perhaps your subject is best presented by audiotape, by photos, by a story.

A shorter project might focus on a specific topic or a short time period in your family history. Family recipes, occupations, anecdotes, and so on can be the basis for preserving your past in print.

Share Your Information

Many of your family members would probably be interested in any information you find. A friend of mine regrets that no one wrote down some of the wonderful dishes that her grandmother cooked. Carrying on her culinary tradition could easily have been an appropriate memorial at family gatherings. Passing down family history helps us appreciate each other more.

Project 27: Calendars

Calendars save our family from miscommunication and scheduling problems before they occur. We still have a few minor lapses, but these generally occur when we forget to write down our activities.

We keep one large monthly calendar at our kitchen desk near the phone. Everyone is expected to write down items as soon as possible and notify me of overlapping events. None of us possess the ability to be in two places at the same time, so this early warning system is important.

If you haven't tried maintaining a calendar as a family project and you are having scheduling difficulties, then this project may solve your problem while providing you with record keeping skills at the same time.

Writing Your Own Schedule

Keep your life organized by scheduling your own activities and appointments even if you don't have a family calendar. Write down important days you want to remember, such as birthdays, holy days, and test days. Include information such as vet visits for your personal pet. Then don't forget to check your calendar each day.

Be considerate and write notes to other family members who need to be informed if you are going to be late to a meal. A day or two ahead, remind the drivers in the family that you need a lift for an appointment on the other side of town. Don't expect others to remember their schedules and yours. Use your calendar to preserve family harmony.

Inspire Yourself

Writing monthly resolutions is another way to use your calendar. Each month is a gift of time. How can you spend your month wisely? Maybe you want to go to confession twice during a month. Perhaps you want to pray a novena for a special intention

Notes:

during the first nine days of the month. Write in the dates as appointments.

Promise yourself that by the end of the month you will have learned to play two new songs on the piano or that you will design a new seasonal wreath for your front door. You can write your resolutions on Post-it® notes and stick the list on the month, so you will see it every time you open your calendar. You will be more likely to keep your good resolutions by setting them down on paper.

Project 28: Action Letters

What is an Action Letter?

An action letter is one written to persuade the audience to take a specific action. You want them to do something to address a situation. Usually, action letters are written to strangers. The writing should be decisive and logical because you want to be taken seriously. Even if you are angry, the letter should be courteous. This kind of writing is not conversational and will require more thought and proofreading than a casual letter to a friend. Don't lose your serious tone through careless grammatical mistakes.

Some Appropriate Situations

We had trouble with our dog chewing on our windowsills. So I bought a bitter spray "guaranteed" to work. The morning after I used it, the dog had taken the largest bite yet out of the windowsill! I called the store and got the name and address of the manufacturer. I didn't have a receipt, but I wrote a letter explaining how much my dog had enjoyed the windowsill. I received a refund, and thankfully, our dog has since grown out of his bad habit.

I am contemplating writing a letter of complaint to a nearby city that officially prohibits school age children from being seen in public even with their parents during school hours. I discovered that they are not enforcing the curfew, but it's still on the books.

My son bought a pair of shorts through a mail order company. After washing them three times, the stitching came loose. So he wrote an explanation to the company and mailed the shorts back, requesting an exchange. He was surprised at how quickly he received a new pair.

Perhaps your neighborhood playground doesn't have any trashcans, and consequently, it's becoming a garbage dump.

Notes:

Write to the homeowner's association or the city to request trashcans, explaining the unsanitary condition of the playground.

Maybe a local theater is showing an anti-Catholic movie, and you would like to register your disapproval in writing. Write a letter to your political representative to support pro-life legislation that is coming up. You may not be able to vote yet, but you will be old enough eventually. You can defend the pro-life position now by letters and later on with voting.

Some Helpful Hints

Confine your letter to one page if possible. State the problem clearly at the beginning. You might explain your reason for getting involved if that is appropriate. Give logical points to support your position or request. State what you want the resolution to be. Proofread the letter carefully. In addition, call for the correct name and address of the responsible party. You don't want your letter to get lost in the wrong department.

What Will Happen to the Letter?

Large companies maintain customer service departments, which will handle your letter. Managers or owners of smaller businesses will read your letter and respond. I have rarely not gotten any response at all. You may receive a form letter, a personal letter, or a phone call.

Many times, people are surprised at responses they receive simply because they wrote a well-reasoned letter of complaint. Having something in writing is often powerful. You may not always change someone else's mind, but sometimes it is morally wrong to keep silent.

Project 29:
Computer Programs

Although you may not have pondered the complexities of computer programming, someone has written line after line of instructions to the computer. Computer programming is real writing. It requires the same skills of organization, questioning, logic, and creativity.

Learning how to write software programs takes time and skill. You must learn a new language with its own rules and symbolic meaning. Yes, programming languages have their own grammar. If you are interested in learning to program, your public library probably has books available on C++, Java, Visual Basic, and other languages. Or you may prefer to take a programming course at your local community college. If you have Microsoft Office, check for Visual Basic Editor on the toolbar under Tools and then Macros. You may also download Visual Studio Express at http://msdn.microsoft.com/downloads/.

Writing Simple Interactive Stories With or Without a Computer

If you have some foundational programming skills, an easy first project is to write an interactive story for younger children. An interactive story allows the audience to add parts to the storyline. Your audience will enjoy filling in the missing parts of the story.

Begin with a simple plot for children. We wrote a program about unusual characters getting on a bus to go to the zoo. When you have finished your story, go back and find places where the audience can "fill in the blank" with an adjective, a noun, a number, a day, a verb, and so on. You will go back and erase these parts of the story. For instance, in our story, the bus driver was (an animal). At the first stop, on a (adjective) Monday morning, he picked up (number) ballet dancers, at the second stop, he picked up a (color) teapot,…

Write the program prompting the audience to key in the nouns, verbs, colors, and numbers at the very beginning of the program. Add any graphics, such as buttons and links or relevant sound clips or images to your story. The audience fills in the missing parts before the story begins, unaware of the storyline. Once the audience has completed the questions, run the program for the complete and often hilarious story they helped create. If you can't write computer programs, you can still write an interactive story on paper. Your "finished" story on paper won't really be finished until you fill in the blanks with your audience's suggestions before you read the story.

This is a good rainy day activity for both writer and audience. It also helps with parts of speech recognition and would be a good instructional aid for young children.

More Computer Programming and Computer-Related Ideas

For a serious computer writing project, you could write a program that would help your family with a problem or decision. For instance, we wrote a math speed drill program written in QBasic, which is not available on Microsoft versions after Windows 98. What about a program that drills your knowledge of Latin vocabulary or of geographical data? Create your own e-cards to send to others and design simple games.

If you have access to the Internet and can get free or inexpensive space, you can write your own web pages or web log as I mentioned earlier in the study guide project. Designing web pages is an exciting area to explore. You can publish your own artwork, poetry, stories, or information for the benefit of many people.

Become acquainted with Excel or other spreadsheet programs, so that you can create a budget to help you save for a future purchase or inventory household possessions for insurance purposes. Do you have a list of your videos and DVDs and CDs in case of theft or a natural disaster? Can you create an electronic worksheet that will automatically calculate your grade point average? You may not consider developing a budget or a grading spreadsheet to be writing, but you are organizing information in

a meaningful and useful way. And organizing data is a valuable writing and thinking skill.

If you have access to PowerPoint, try designing slide presentations for fun or as a study aid. You can write a story that unfolds slide by slide with sounds and animation. A PowerPoint presentation can help you review math formulas step-by-step or remember key dates in World History. Yes, it can be a lot of work to develop a PowerPoint presentation, but if you tie it in with your course work, you will be learning necessary subject material while you are improving your computer skills. You will probably find yourself needing to know and use PowerPoint if you enroll in a college speech class.

Because computers are an integral part of our lives, learning as much about them as you can is a smart educational decision.

Resources:

Project 30: Radio and Video Production

Radio and television are both interesting and powerful methods of communicating ideas. Radio and television productions require writing, speaking, and art skills. They are opportunities to bring together various communication skills for the community.

Furthermore, many radio and television productions consistently disregard spiritual values. If we are interested in improving the quality of these productions, we can't ignore opportunities to suggest better material or to create it ourselves.

Suggestions

If you do not want to spend the effort actually producing a program, you may still be able to suggest subjects to radio and television stations. You can present a suggestion to your local radio or television station as an action letter, but the more suggestive details you outline, the better chance you have of persuading the station manager or the advertiser to consider your idea.

For example, you may have heard an offensive clothing ad on the radio or television. In the case of advertising, write to the store, or their headquarters if it's a chain. Explain why the ad is offensive. Suggest a better idea in detail.

You might want to use a separate sheet of paper for the suggestion because you are presenting two different points to the store. You don't want the two ideas—first that the ad is offensive and second that you have a better idea—to get mixed up. If the two points are not crowded together, the reader will be more likely to consider each one separately. Paint a clear picture of the new ad with your words.

Instead of merely complaining to a television station that an episode about homeschoolers was obviously written by someone who knows nothing about homeschooling, suggest that real homeschoolers are consulted before writers begin to lose touch with reality. Make a suggestion for a new episode that gives at least a few real facts about homeschooling. List several facts. Yes, television is imaginary, but even imaginary plots have to be grounded in some reality.

Creating Your Own Productions

You might enjoy the challenge of producing a radio or television program on your own. Maybe you would like to explore it as a career possibility, use the opportunity to improve your communications skills, design an ad for a local business or charitable group, develop an educational program, make a promotional program to highlight a friend's singing ability, or create a gift video for family and friends to enjoy.

Planning Your Production

What kind of equipment do you have available? Dust off the camcorder and the tape recorder. You don't have to begin with fancy equipment. A tape recorder and microphone will get you going. Perhaps you could borrow or rent a camcorder if you don't own one. Sets and props don't matter if you are doing an audio production, although you do want an area that isn't too noisy. A ringing telephone in the kitchen could interrupt your poetry recitation.

Ask yourself lots of questions. What kind of show or program do you want to produce? Will it be humorous or serious? Do you want to do a documentary or a fictional piece? How long will it be? Who will be the audience? Who would be most interested in your idea—senior citizens, children, parents, athletes, musicians? Plan your work based upon the answers to these questions.

Discuss your written plan with any helpers you may require. They will want to know what they are getting involved in.

Write the first draft of the program guideline or script. Then ask yourself a few more questions. What do you need to make this work? More performers? Sound effects? Music? Props? Costumes? Should you scale back your production, making it more focused?

Keep discussing the project as it develops with your helpers. Be open to their ideas.

Write the final script. Rehearse the script a few times.

Get Comfortable with Your Equipment

If you have never operated a camcorder or audio equipment before, practice using it. Get comfortable with turning it off and on. Play with the zoom lens. Play with the volume control.

Ideas for a Small Production

If you are just beginning to use audiovisual equipment, start very small. You can produce an instructional aid for a young child, record a story with sound effects for a party or family get together, create a unique audio birthday "card" for a friend, or tape a selection of your best poems as an audio scrapbook.

Here's a possibility for a simple instructional aid. Help your brother or sister learn a Scripture verse with an audiotape. Select a verse. How can you present the verse? Should you put it to music? Chant it? What will help the listener remember the verse?

You could read the verse slowly, and then inform the listener to repeat short phrases after you, pausing to give the listener time. You could say the verse slowly three times, and then keep repeating it with a different word left out each time, asking the listener to fill in the missing word. How long should the lesson run? Ten to fifteen minutes might be a good length. Time your script.

Evaluate your work by letting a child play the tape. Did you give enough information about the lesson and how to use the tape? Did you speak clearly? Did you leave enough time for the listener to respond? Did the child learn the verse?

If you want to produce an audio birthday "card," what format will you use—a traditional letter, a storyline, a dialogue, poetry, song, or a speech?

Maybe your best friend moved away recently. You could tape record a journal of what you have been doing since she left. Maybe you are going to visit a relative far away. Tape record an interview while you are visiting to share with other family members back home.

You can tape a short letter several times and choose the best production. Listen to your results carefully and determine if anything is missing. Don't expect a perfect production on the first take. Be willing to revise and correct.

Stepping Through a Major Production

Let's walk through a major video production. You have decided to help your karate instructor by filming a promotional video. He wants a short five to seven minute tape he can show to parents and students who come in for information. But he doesn't know what information to present.

You begin jotting down notes. What is important to parents and their children? They probably want to see how a class is run and what skills their children will learn.

You decide to show brief clips of the beginning, middle, and end of a class. A dramatic opening of a board breaking would get your audience's attention immediately.

Watching the class, you realize that it is too large for good shots. You won't need sound effects other than the student and instructor's normal commands and responses, but you need to be in position for the microphone to pick up both commands and responses without picking up distracting noises from the parking lot. You discuss your ideas with the instructor and request the help of three students of various ages.

Then you speak with the selected students, asking for their cooperation. You tell them exactly what you expect on the tape. They will begin the class as usual, and you will tape a short scene. Then they will begin the class again, so you can take another angle. And so on. A five or six minute video can require from thirty minutes to an hour of shooting.

Editing Your Video

You can edit the tape with sophisticated technology, if you have access to home editing equipment. If you are volunteering your services to a small business, the business owner may want to pay someone for a professional edit. In that case, detailed notes will tell the professional editor which scenes you want to keep, although a professional editor may find a better combination of scenes because of his experience.

In addition, you can carefully edit as you shoot, which is difficult for amateurs. The timing has to be right from one shot to the next.

Your last option is to use two VCRs (or one VCR and the camcorder) and a television to copy only the shots you want onto

Resources:

99

a second blank tape. See your camcorder instruction manual for connecting the camcorder to the VCR. Then run the rough draft on the camcorder while taping only the sections you want to keep onto the VCR tape.

If your edited tape jumps at the joins, you may have to black up the blank tape. To black up a tape, place it in the camcorder *with the lens cap on* while recording. This process is supposed to synchronize the electronic pulses, making your joins smoother. However, I spoke with someone who had done editing like this, and she never blacked up any tapes.

Editing is slow, careful work. If you don't like the results, remember that you still have all the shots on the rough draft video.

Don't be surprised if you find annoying mistakes and if the scenes don't flow smoothly. Professional videographers have resources for fading, dissolving, and wiping scenes that you don't.

Make a note of mistakes that you can correct, and either re-shoot, or don't criticize your first effort so harshly. You will do better next time. Even professional films contain mistakes, such as a plane flying over a medieval courtyard or the hero's wet head of hair that miraculously dries from one moment to the next.

A Few More Ideas

You can use audio and video in a variety of ways. You could design a video anniversary "card" for your parents. Include old photographs, old songs, and family mementos from their wedding and first year together.

Tape seasonal greetings to send to faraway friends through a well-organized program of conversation, a play, poetry, and song. Videotape your vacation to show to homeschooled friends. You can record and narrate the educational parts of your vacation to historic sites.

Write your own mystery story, videotape it, and then invite your friends over for a sleuthing party.

Make a home inventory of possessions using video for insurance purposes. Preserve important parts of a family reunion on video. If you want to sell your house, make a short video of the good points to play for prospective buyers. Get up on the roof to show its condition. Take close-ups of any unique areas of the house, such as a new ceramic floor or the great landscaping.

Create a Public Service Announcement

You may have seen a television spot that looks like a very short commercial, but it isn't selling anything. This is called a public service announcement or PSA. A seasonal PSA reminds people to set their clocks ahead for Daylight Savings Time. The electric company often warns people not to fly kites near light poles through PSAs.

Design and send a thirty second public service announcement on video or audio to a local television or radio station. They are required by law to donate a certain amount of time for these, and while they may not accept your homemade production, they might want to find out more about your idea. Contact the director of public relations at a local station once you have developed your PSA.

Additional Help

If you are interested in learning more about video or radio production, check with your local community college. If it offers classes, you will have access to equipment and more technical help for a reasonable cost.

Resources:

Extra: Communicate With Your Community

Find ways to use your writing, drawing, and speaking skills to benefit others. You probably belong to many groups—a parish, a neighborhood, a club, a homeschooling organization—that could benefit from your skills.

Perhaps you could write short book reviews to introduce parishioners to good Catholic materials for your parish bulletin each month. Call your parish secretary and ask.

Businesses may send you marketing surveys. Have you ever completed a comment card in a restaurant when you received excellent service? Mystery shoppers are reimbursed or paid for posing as customers in order to critique services in various businesses. Maybe a friend has a shop that could benefit from handwritten or computer generated signs.

Small business owners who can't afford professional services may be willing to let you gain some experience by writing and taping advertisements. Advertising is expensive because of the cost of audio or video production and the air time. Radio time is less expensive than television. And newspaper ads can be the least expensive way to advertise depending upon the size of the ad. Call the station or paper, asking for the advertising manager to get their rates.

You may also be able to provide business owners, charitable organizations, or your parish with promotional flyers, brochures, and press releases. A press release is newsworthy information sent to the mass media. It's either an introduction to a story or feature that the editor may want to follow up on or a complete article of an event, giving the vital facts about who, what, when, where, and why.

Word processing software, such as Microsoft Word, has step-by-step tutorials to teach you how to set up brochures and press releases.

People need to communicate, and writing well is an effective way to reach out to others and build a better community.

Additional Information

Appendix One: Plot Situations

If you are stumped for a storyline, review this abbreviated list, paraphrased from *The Thirty-Six Dramatic Situations* by Georges Polti.

1. A persecutor or adverse situation causes a petitioner to appeal for help from authority—A penniless juggler runs from a mob and grabs the altar cloth in an abbey church claiming sanctuary.

2. An unfortunate is delivered by a rescuer—An angel frees Peter from prison.

3. An avenger pursues a criminal—Jacob's sons kill Hamor's men in revenge for the kidnapping of their sister Dinah.

4. Family vengeance—King Solomon orders his brother Adonijah slain for his political intrigue.

5. Flight and pursuit—The Holy Family flees from Herod's soldiers.

Writing lists:

6. A man-made or natural disaster—Rome conquers Jerusalem and enslaves the people.

7. Undeserved cruelty or misfortune falls upon the innocent—the Passion and Crucifixion of Christ

8. The oppressed revolt against a tyrant—The American colonists revolt against English rule.

9. A leader or group attempts a daring enterprise—The Apostles preach the Good News in Jerusalem against the orders of the Sanhedrin.

10. Kidnapping and recapture—Abram frees his nephew Lot from warring kings.

11. Search for the answer to a deadly puzzle—The hobbit Bilbo Baggins played a riddling game with Gollum, hoping to be led out of danger if he won.

12. A person tries to obtain help or a treasure by persuasion, deception, or force—St. Paul eloquently debates with many in Athens because he is exasperated at the number of idols in the city.

13. The results of hatred or jealousy within a family—Cain slays Abel.

14. A person suffers from his own lack of wisdom—King Midas loses his daughter because of his greed for gold.

15. A person sacrifices himself for a great cause—the Passion and Crucifixion of Christ.

16. A person is asked or forced to sacrifice a loved one for the good of the community or for God's favor—God asks Abraham to sacrifice Isaac.

17. A rivalry between a superior power and an inferior one—David fights Goliath.

18. Obstacles to love or marriage—Jacob is tricked into marrying Leah and must work seven more years to win Rachel as his wife.

19. An enemy is loved or aided—Rahab saves the lives of Joshua's spies who plan to conquer Jericho.

20. The results of ambition—Men build the tower of Babel, and God scatters them and confuses their language.

21. Struggle against God—Jonah refuses to obey God's commands until he is swallowed by a great fish.

22. False suspicions—most mystery stories revolve around false accusations.

23. Repentance—Saul repents of his persecutions of the Church and seeks baptism from Ananias.

24. The death of loved ones—the Passion and Crucifixion of Christ.

Resources:

Appendix Two: How-to Books

If you can't find the book listed, use the library call numbers to locate similar resources.

Emberley, Ed. *Great Thumbprint Drawing Book.* Boston: Little, Brown and Co., 1977. (Library call no. Juvenile 760) Easy cartooning method useful for making cards, decorating signs, and so on.

Fishman, Stephen. *The Copyright Handbook: How to Protect and Use Written Works.* Berkeley: Nolo Press, 1996. (Library call no. 346.7304) A legal self-help book for registering your own copyrights and obtaining permission to use others' writings.

Guthrie, Donna and Nancy Bentley. *The Young Producer's Video Book: How to Write, Direct, and Shoot Your Own Video.* Brookfield, Connecticut: The Millbrook Press, 1995. (Library call no. Juvenile 791.54) Technical information and ideas.

Holm, Kirsten C. *The Writer's Market.* Cincinnati: F&W Publications, 1999. (Library call no. 029 WRI) Exhaustive guide to publishing.

Irvine, Joan. *How to Make Super Pop-ups.* New York: Morrow Junior Books, 1992. (Library call no. Juvenile 741.5) Learn how to design greeting cards and books.

Manual of Style. Chicago University Press. Look for the latest edition. (Library call no. 655.2) How to proofread and prepare your writing for publication.

Pellowski, Anne. *The Storytelling Handbook: A Young People's Collection of Unusual Tales and Helpful Hints on How to Tell Them.* New York: Simon & Schuster, 1995. (Library call no. Juvenile 372.64) Guide to finding an interesting story, various ways to learn and perform stories.

Phillips, Ellen. *Shocked, Appalled, and Dismayed: How to Write Letters of Complaint that Get Results.* New York: Vintage, 1997. (Library call no. 371.3)

Squires, Malcolm. *Video Camcorder School: A practical guide to making great home videos.* Pleasantville, New York: Quarto Publishing, 1992. (Library call no. 778.59) An adult guide to handling a camcorder.

Resources:

Internet Addresses

Genealogy Records, Worksheets, and Tips

- http://www.usgenweb.com/ (A non-commercial site that includes tips for getting started, archives of public records, tombstone surveys, and forms to download.)
- http://www.vitalrec.com (Research birth, marriage, and other public records within all fifty states.)
- http://www.ancestry.com (A database for name searches)

Copyright Information

- http://lcweb.loc.gov/copyright (The Library of Congress site gives the basics of copyrighting and how to register for a copyright.)

The Writer's Digest

- http://writersdigest.com (At this site, you can check out books and magazines for writers and find information on general writing contests and conferences.)

Notes:

Supplies

We usually buy writing supplies from office supply warehouses, such as Office Depot and Office Max. Here is a list of what we try to keep on hand:

Felt tip pens in black and blue

Permanent black marker

Ballpoint pens & pencils

Letter stencils

Stick-on letters

Poster paints

Felt in various colors for book covers and banners

Sculpey Clay—can be used for 3-D lettering and imprinting

Rubber stamps and three colors of inkpads

Calligraphy pens and ink

Computer paper

White card stock and envelopes—Geocard Smooth Card Stock and Geographics Greeting Card Envelopes are about the least expensive we have found.

Unlined and lined index cards—the large size makes inexpensive postcards, and smaller ones are good for instructional aids and place cards

Various sizes of blank stickers—for labeling and name tags

Post it Notes

Message pads

Bound Composition Notebooks—for writing you want to keep as the spiral bound notebooks tend to tear easily

Perforated notepads—for scratch paper or temporary lists

Appendix Three: Copyrights and Fair Use

The purpose of copyright laws is to protect the author's original creative work, but titles, ideas, and facts cannot be copyrighted. It is a crime to steal an author's expressions, unless your writing is considered "fair use."

Fair use means limited quotation without written permission usually for nonprofit educational reasons. News reporting, criticism, learning activities, and teaching generally fall under the fair use rule.

If you are writing a book review, you can certainly quote a few lines without having to contact the publisher. You do want to acknowledge the author even if your use of someone's creative expression is considered fair use.

Some old songs are now part of public domain, which means they are no longer copyrighted. Parodies of any kind are considered fair use. "Happy Birthday" is still under copyright according to one reference book I read, but, of course, singing it for your family is not considered a crime.

As an example of fair use for teaching, I did not write to the publisher of *The Thirty-Six Dramatic Situations*. I also didn't use quotation marks because I didn't use the author's direct expressions. I paraphrased, acknowledging the source. Although the idea that there are only thirty-six possible plots may be Georges Polti's, he cannot copyright ideas. If you were to find his book, you would probably see that many of the words are similar or the same, but my list is much simpler.

If you think your quotations have gone beyond fair use, please write to the publisher for permission. If you don't know the publisher's address, ask your librarian for the *Literary Market Place* or the *Gale Directory of Publications*.

Appendix Four: Simple Grammar Rules

For the Convenience of Our Readers:

1. Capitalize names of people. (Adam and Eve)

2. Capitalize names of places. (United States and the White House)

3. Capitalize names of books and music. (The Bible and Ave Maria)

4. Capitalize the first word of each sentence. (The bird sang.)

5. Punctuate the end of each sentence. (Who knocks? I knocked.)

6. Use apostrophes for contractions. (It's cold. You're early.)

7. Use 's most of the time to show possession. (the dog's fleas and Tom's book but its fleas and his book)

8. Use a comma in a series of three or more words. (red, white, and blue)

9. Use a comma and a conjunction to join two sentences together. (The cat hissed, and the dog barked.)

6

DRAWING

Writing Samples

Diary Excerpts – Cathy age 7

Jan. 7 I tack musick lesens. At homeschool. I play the recorder. Do you want to here a soing. OK the titl is. Long-short March. Long-short march Long-short march paly the short notes one two three four Long short march Long short march Long notes soar.

Jan 8 My mom says her favrite animal is a rabbit. Rabbits are ok. But I like horses. Even though we have bifrint favrit animals we still love ech uthr.

Fed. 4 I like fish swiming in water. I wuld like to have a pet fish. But my mom says no. I still hope I get a fish.

Feb. 12 Mary is are mom. She is Jesus's mom to. She is the mom of God. I love Mary and Jesus.

(These entries selected from the first two months of 1992 were uncorrected. The diary was a birthday gift intended to be a record of her seven year old thoughts and to show how her writing was progressing. As you can see, she confuses her "b's" and "d's." Most of her entries also include drawings. Samples of her more recent diary entries appear near the end of the writing samples section.)

Our Dog

I know a dog & he is Mattie. He is cute & not fat & when he first came here that is a story that you shall hear.

Our story begins when we are going to go to the pound but my mom's mom & dad had a party & we needed to go. So the next day we went to a different church which was close to the pound.

After the Mass we went to the pound. After a search we saw a Lab. But I thought that it was too big so for my sake we looked again & saw a dog (Mattie) & dad asked about him & dad signed the papers& bought him.

The next day we picked him up & all he did was sniff the floor & ate. Bed time.

Mom put him to bed but he did not fit in the bed that mom made for him. The next day I woke up &

I saw Cathy playing with him & he played alot but I had school to do so I

did my school & played with him. Wen Dad came home he ran around the room at 100 miles an hour

& jumped on dad & at suppere time he begged which dad did not like very much.

& he lived happily ever after.

the end
by Anthony age 8

(This is a true story written as a memory article about an exciting day for my son. We corrected the capitalization and left most of the other mistakes, while saving his eight year old expression and his computer formatting.)

top ace teens

STARRING:
BETSY & ANTHONY
AS: JANIA & JACAN ORS

Scene 2: blast off

[step in to the space ship it will be two couches pushed together]

B. turn on the thruster
A. done
B. engines
A. done
B. secure your webbing
A. done
A & B. BLAST OFF!!!!

SCENE THREE:ATTACKED

A.we are having thruster problems
B. let me see
A. looks like we will need your expertis
B. looks like we will need new thruster boxs
A. WE'RE UNDER ATTACK!!!!!!!!!!!!!!
B. DO SOMETHING!!!!
A. LIKE WHAT?
B. HEAD FOR THE NEAREST PLANET
A. WHICH ONE
B. THE GREEN ONE
A. THAT'S WHERE WE CAME FROM
B. THEN THE BLUE ONE
C.Abandon ship abandon ship
A.what's the hurry
(black out end of part one.)

(The two stars—ages 9 and 10—collaborated on this play, which premiered one evening at home. The play was about 30 minutes long. The audience gave it a thumbs up. This was not a writing assignment, but they put a lot of effort into it.)

Resources:

Notes:

Buying My Own Clothes

—by Betsy age 10

About five months ago, Mom and Dad decided that they needed to teach us the value of money. On the fifteenth of each month they gave us fifty-five dollars to spend. I handle my money like this: five dollars [10%] goes to the church, three dollars [6%] goes to our base ball fund, usually ten dollars [20%] for clothes, the rest of the money [64%] I put in the bank.

I find that it is a lot harder to buy my own clothes then to have some one else do it. Why is it harder to buy something with your own money than to have some one else buy it? 1)If your own money is being spent, then generally you are more careful of what you spend it on. 2) If you have ten dollars and thirty eight cents, and you want candy, you might be trying to find the cheapest brand you like, or you might go without to save your money for other things. 3) If you want designer clothes, you might consider asking for them as a Christmas present before you go out and buy them . . .

(Elizabeth wrote a two page editorial on how she handled her money. The purpose of the assignment was to make her think about her spending, saving, and charitable donations.)

Star Family on Lux Four

Betsy Garant age 10

Sorry Mom I know I'm late. No, we just started. Okay. She sat down with her brothers who just made it in to at the wooden table and served herself some of the potatoes and green beans and barley meal they were having. Beep! Beep! Beep! Leslie would you get that her mom said. It's for you. Okay, no problem. Her younger brother whispered something about "her beau" but she ignored him. He was always teasing her about the calls she got. She hit the button on the message wall that said receive. And this message flashed across the screen: Leslie, do not forget the meeting tonight on the roof tonight after supper. Kevin.

She hit the return button on the wall and wrote: All right Kevin. I'll be there when I can.

She walked back to the table and sat down. Gerald her older brother said. What was that about? Was it from your partner? I don't have a partner Gerald. How could it be from my partner if I don't have one? You don't have to get ruffled, I just asked a question. Leslie told her mom and dad that someone she talked to at school said he had a ratio beam for her data pad. She would like to go after dinner and see what it was he wanted for it if they said it was okay. They told her she could go.

(An excerpt from a ten page science fiction story written for entertainment. I made a few spelling corrections. In reading her story two years later, she remarked that quotations come in handy. Although it was not an assignment, this would be a good story for proofreading now because she can see obvious mistakes.)

Trampoline Rules

by Cathy, Elizabeth, and Anthony Garant

1. You cannot jump off the trampoline. You must slide down gently.

2. You cannot wear glasses while bouncing on the trampoline.

3. No sharp objects in pockets or hands. No watch, belt, shoes or socks while bouncing.

4. No hard shoving or bouncing when two people are on together.

5. No disparaging comments on someone else's trick.

6. No flips.

7. Only two people can bounce at one time.

(The children presented me with these reassuring rules in 1998 after I finally agreed to let them have a trampoline. I gave them credit for a writing assignment and common sense.)

Wind

Wind, wind,
Wind can be a soft, a gentle breeze
That cools my head-ache.
It can be strong and hard,
Making me want to run around and shout:
Wind, wind, wind!

—Cathy age 11

Matti's Lullaby

Go to sleep, to sleep my Matti,
Drift away to dream-lands bay,
There you shall swim and play.
Go to sea, to sleep, my Matti,
Go to sea, to sleep, Matthias,
Drift away to dream-lands bay,
There you shall swim and play.

—Cathy age 11

Resources:

Answering Machine Messages

"G'day, this is the Garant answering service. If you know who we are, you'll get the Aussie accent, but if you don't you won't. Oh yeah, don't forget to leave a message after the tone. Thanks."

"Lift your eyes to the wonders of the Lord during this year of Jubilee. Please leave your message after the tone."

(These are scripts written and performed by Anthony. He practiced his Aussie accent for a few days before the G'day script. He's gotten some interesting reactions from callers.)

Song

By Anthony age 10

> A little bit of my guardian angel while I sleep
>
> A little bit of Jesus while I'm awake
>
> A little bit of Mary while I pray
>
> My patron saint all day _____
>
> A little bit of every saint that I need
>
> A little bit of St. Joseph in my need
>
> A little bit of St. Michael by my side
>
> The Holy Spirit on my mind . . .

(This is Anthony's rendition of a contemporary song that he decided to change. His sisters provide the backup vocals.)

Anthony's Packing List — age 10

	Packed to leave	Packed to come home
Shorts		
Jeans		
Shirts		
Shoes		

(This is my son's list to help him remember what to pack and then to make sure he is bringing everything back home.)

Resources:

BLESSED MIGUEL PRO

by Anthony Garant age 11

Miguel Pro was born January the 13th in Mexico. He was very much like me in the sense that he was very mischievous and he frequently annoyed everyone with his jokes and sense of humor. Miguel became a priest after Mexico became anti-Catholic. He would disguise himself as a beggar or whatever disguises were necessary to get to people who wanted their baby baptized or the people in jail who wanted Holy Communion. He was accused of trying to kill the Mexican President and was betrayed by the police and sentenced to death without a trial. He was shot by the firing squad, and bravely refusing a blindfold, died saying "Viva Cristo Rey", "Long live Christ the King."

(Anthony's Confirmation teacher gave him this assignment in April 2000, which I agreed to accept as his writing for the week. This is the corrected version.)

Notes:

Elizabeth's New Year's 2000 Resolutions

This year I am going to get my room set up the way I want it.

Earn 2000 golden pennies

Finish writing a novel

Finish two songbooks for the piano

Learn to juggle 3 beanbags

Learn several card tricks

Finish reading the Brother Cadfael mysteries

Learn how to read music

And grow a garden

Diary Excerpts—Cathy age 12

Day two,
Dear Dad, We got up at about 6:30. We went downstairs to eat breakfast. Met Grandma and Grandpa on the way down. Oh, I forgot to tell you, They were traveling with Aunt Jean, and they stayed at the Holiday Inn in Crestview too.

We made it to Wakulla all right and walked into the lobby where we met Grandma and Grandpa, Aunt Jean, Uncle Robert and Co., and my cousin Jeff B. (I know I did not spell that right) with his two daughters, Rachel and Katy.

****

The nature trails at Wakulla are very interesting. They had all kinds of plants, including Poison Ivy. (No one got it) We also saw butterflies, centipedes, and mosquitoes. We even saw an alligator. We were walking on a trail that dead-ended in a swamp. We looked around and saw the back of an alligator about a hundred feet away.

****

We were about to watch a movie while recovering from our walk, when Aunt Jean asked us if we wanted to go swimming. So we got on our swim suits and headed for the water. The water in the Swimming area was very clear, and very cold!

I swam for a little bit, then went over to a two-level diving platform they had. I did not jump from the highest platform dispite Robby's derogatory remarks. Aunt Jean pulled something in her leg when she jumped, and Katy really hurt herself doing a cannon ball.

(These are excerpts from an uncorrected travel journal. Cathy was very unhappy that my husband could not travel with us to a family reunion, and so someone suggested that she write a journal to give to him when she returned. She wrote something almost every day of the weeklong trip.)

Resources:

121

My Will

I, Catherine Garant, do hereby make my will and give my worldly goods in the year of Our Lord, the 22nd of March, 1998 A.D.

Being sane of mind and sound of body I here by allot 10 percent of all my money to be donated to the Church, and another 10 percent for the homeless or other charitable organization.

The other 80 percent is to be given to my mother and father. My useable clothing is to be divided in two, one half is to go to Elizabeth, the other is to be donated to the Salvation Army. Elizabeth also gets half of my books.

My toys and the other half of my books will go to Anthony. My jewelry is to be divided between Mom and Elizabeth.

My dad gets my mementos. (i.e. pictures, cards, pict. albums, baby bag and quilt, ticket stubs, certificates, et cetera.)
This also includes my First Holy Communion ring.

Matthias (the dog) is to have my bed sheets. (One at a time, though, so that they last longer.)

Any computer games that I own are for everyone in the family to play. Also, any friends and/or relatives that wish may have a lock of my hair.

All my useable organs are to be donated to a hospital.

—Catherine A. Garant age 12

(My daughter decided to write her will after both of her grandfathers were hospitalized for major surgery. She updates it once a year or so.)

Dreams by Cathy age 14

I would like to gain maturity, so that I need not scowl or use harsh words on my family.

I would like to be worthy of respect.

I would like to visit at least a few old castles.

I would like to draw at least one beautiful picture of someone.

I would like to be able to dance.

I would like to know my Guardian Angel's name.

Resources:

Dreams by Elizabeth age 11

I want to finish a novel.

I want to learn more grammar.

I want to get my room painted.

I want to become famous.

(These are lists of future aspirations, which we all wrote and shared with each other as a writing assignment in 1999. It's interesting to see how our dreams change from year to year. Elizabeth did get her room painted, and Cathy learned the foxtrot.)

Daily Petitions

by the Garant Family

We pray for world peace.

We pray for Aunt Jane.

We pray for our family that it may grow closer to God.

In thanksgiving for 3 new mountain bikes.

We pray for everyone providing meals for the — family.

For a speciale intention

That I will enjoy school (evre minet of it) and do ecsepshunule well on math.

We pray for the victims of the school massacre in CO

That St. Thomas will help us with our schoolwork

That dire Mary and Jesus and Josef, St. Anthony and my gardean angul will plese get me a pin-pall

For Smokey, Basil, and Fiver (our baby rabbits that died)

Birthday blessings for L.R. and D.G.

We ask for comfort and healing for L.T. and her family.

In thanksgiving for our vacation in Galveston and that we found the right church for our pilgrimage prayers

(Excerpts from our Daily Petitions notebook. These are not graded or corrected and are voluntary.)

The Rabbit Solution

Question: How can we transport 3 full grown rabbits, one large two medium, during a 3-5 hour car trip during the hottest part of the day without inconveniencing anybody?

Answer: The answer is not easy. Assuming that each rabbit must be transported separately I have come up with these solutions.

1. We have at least 2 small milk crates. If we put a plastic trash bag and half a newspaper in the bottom we could put them on the floor in the front seat of the cars.

2. We have a trash can. If we leave the lid off and seat someone in the middle of the car to hold it steady it could contain 1 rabbit.

3. We have a small cage outside. The cage might fit on the floor in the back seat.

—by Elizabeth Garant age 12

(A very practical assignment! All three rabbit owners came up with different ideas and discussed their solutions.)

Thrift Shop Donation List
For Tax Deductions

by Cathy Garant age 15

1 pair lady's shoes

2 stuffed toys

2 twin comforters

2 lady's purses

1 child's T-shirt

1 lady's skirt

1 girl's cardigan

2 lady's dresses

1 lady's jumper

2 lady's pants

1 knick-knack

(Instead of holding garage sales, we donate items to the thrift stores and keep a record for tax purposes. This is a practical lesson that I assign about 2-3 times a year. It promotes careful record-keeping and spelling.)

The Library Compromise

Catherine (age 15) and Elizabeth Garant (age 12) in order to provide the family with a library and some peace and quiet at the same time, here ratify this compromise for living in the same room.

I. Both must agree to any changes to this compromise before the changes may be ratified.

II. Both shall respect the privacy and rights of each other, treating each other with love, respect, and consideration at all times.

III. Items acceptable to both parties under the respective headings of Furniture, Decoration, and Stuff: dresser, bunk, both desks, mirror, Betsy's hamper, and Cathy's alarm clock; crucifix, poster, and calendar; Legos, art supplies, memorabilia, stuffed animals, and plants.

IV. Both girls shall wash their sheets together each week, that they may share the top bunk. The person inhabiting the top bunk shall be responsible for the cleanliness of the floor and mirror throughout the week, while the inhabitant of the bottom bunk shall likewise be in charge of dusting and turning off the alarm clock.

V. With acceptable exceptions, both parties shall rise in the morning at 5:55 a.m., and begin preparations to retire at 9:00 p.m.

VI. Both parties agree to keep any items of stuff not intended for the floor (notably clothing) off the floor. They also agree to leave the windowsill unfurnished.

VII. Both agree to paint the room with base coat and (possibly) trimmings.

(This was an unexpected proposal for a change in living arrangements when the girls wanted a separate library/study area at the beginning of 2000. I accepted it as a writing assignment.)